The Authors

Derek Biddle has had many years' experience in personnel management, industrial relations and management development in industry and commerce, both in the UK and overseas. After early experience in the Merchant Navy and then in the Fleet Air Arm, he qualified as an engineer and worked in the manufacturing industry. It was here that he discovered that the people parts of the job were for him the most interesting and productive and he decided to specialize in personnel management and training. He gained his MSc at the University of Bath in 1972 and his PhD in 1976. He is also a Fellow of the Institute of Personnel Management. Before joining his present company, The London Life Association Ltd, where he is a practising manager, he was an Assistant Director of Studies at Roffey Park Management College. He has published widely on people aspects of management, is married with three children and spends most of his spare time sailing.

Robin Evenden has a management development and training consultancy. He is an Associate of Will Denn Resources, Horsham, with which he runs open courses in the areas covered by this book. In addition, he is an External Tutor for Strathclyde Business School. He was previously the Senior Tutor and later the Deputy Director of Roffey Park Management College. During the period when it established its reputation for people management training, Robin was responsible for all its courses and consultancy. He has trained many thousands of managers and has over twenty years' management, consultancy and training experience from shop floor to boardroom, and from basic skills to university post-graduate seminars. His current work involves converting specialists to managers, orientation programmes for those responding to role changes, management skill repertoire development and team building. A graduate of the London School of Economics and an industrial sociologist, he is a Fellow of both the British Institute of Management and the Institute of Training and Development. Robin is married, has four children and runs marathons from time to time.

HUMAN ASPECTS
OF
MANAGEMENT

Second Edition

Derek Biddle
Robin Evenden

Cartoons by Dennis Baker

Institute of Personnel Management

Acknowledgements

We would like to acknowledge the support of our many friends and colleagues over the years, whose creativity, ideas and training skills have helped us develop this book. Special mention should be made of Julie Archer, Dave Barker, Neil Clark of Process Training Associates and David Hughes, for the contribution discussions with them have made to the additions and innovations in the second edition. Finally, none of it would have been possible without the prompting and typing of Lyn Plummer, who provided us with unstinting and skilful effort.

Phototypeset by Wessex Typesetters, Frome
and printed in Great Britain by Dotesios Ltd,
Trowbridge, Wiltshire

British Library Cataloguing Publication Data
Biddle, Derek
  Human aspects of management.—2nd ed.
  1. Personnel management—Manuals
  I. Title   II. Evenden, Robin
  III. Institute of Personnel Management
  658.3
  ISBN 0–85292–395–3

Contents

Preface to the second edition

The book is intended for practising managers and students of management. It deals with perennial issues and problems which arise when working with people and our work with many hundreds of managers demonstrates the continued and increasing relevance of the *Human Aspects of Management*.

The new edition has been significantly enlarged and includes four important new chapters which reflect developments in the role of the manager as we move into the last decade of the twentieth century.

'Managing learning, development and performance' deals with the manager's growing responsibility to help individuals enhance performance-related skills. It looks at the need to assist people to grow, both in confidence and the capacity to work well in situations of change, two vital facets of working in modern employment. The chapter contains new and original material on performance coaching styles and delegation.

Other new chapters are 'Making a difference: personal power and influence' and 'Handling interpersonal conflict'. They stress the need to influence through personal behaviour, rather than structural power, particularly in roles which involve functional or matrix management or 'client' relationships. They aim to help the reader understand the choices available when handling the potential conflicts between the needs of self and others.

The chapter on work groups now includes a summary of approaches to intergroup relationships. Another new chapter, 'Understanding people' includes many of the key parts of the first edition's 'Managing individuals: behaviour, attitudes, perception and personality', and some material from the 'Motivation' chapter. 'Meetings' has been expanded to include more and different information on effective contribution skills, and 'Interviewing' has additional material covering listening skills. The 'Change' chapter has new material on personal change and choices.

The second edition has many new 'activity plans' and continues the successful approach of encouraging learning not just by reading about concepts and techniques, but by reflection upon experience and trying things out in practice.

List of figures

Introduction

If you are a T-type manager or through study are aspiring to
become one, then this book is for you. A T-type manager is a
technocrat who has acquired technical, thing or task knowledge
by experience, education or training. Our aim is to provide an
opportunity for self development in complementary knowledge
and skills in the one area of responsibility common to all managers:
the human aspects of management.

The most demanding and difficult part of the manager's job is
managing people and relationships. It is this more than anything
else which determines success or failure, yet it is frequently
neglected. The book will give you the chance to increase your
knowledge and awareness of yourself and others, as well as the
opportunity to develop important managerial skills of analysis,
diagnosis and action concerning people at work.

Human Aspects of Management asks the following questions and
we hope will help you find answers that are appropriate for you:

What am I doing when I manage?
How do I manage other people?
Do I understand myself and others?
How can I help people learn and develop?
What creates good and bad relationships?
How do I influence others?
How do I handle conflict?
What is communication without words?
What helps success in face to face contact?
What makes meetings effective?
How can a group's performance be influenced?
How should change be handled?
What helps people to work well?

The book does not specifically broach the subject of trade union relationships, which merit and frequently receive special treatment elsewhere. However, we think that the interpersonal, psychological and sociological factors explored are relevant to all aspects of organizational life, including industrial relations.

You will be invited to do more than read this book. It will be suggested that you try the activity plans designed to bring the text to life in a practical and creative way. Some activities are questionnaires; some are observational games and experiments; others mean harnessing what you know already and building upon that knowledge.

The activity plans may provide constructively amusing and interesting personal development for the practising manager or an integrated sequence of serious exercises for the examination student who wishes to learn the essential theory, at the same time as making sense of the realities of management. The activities can be undertaken by the reader alone, although many of them lend themselves to shared learning with another or a group.

We hope that *Human Aspects of Management* will increase your range of choices in the fascinating and challenging business of managing with and through other people.

1 Managing with people

This chapter looks at some ideas about management including its purpose, what it does and solving problems with people. A human aspects framework and checklist is described which also serves as an outline for the book.

In common with all chapters, an activity plan is suggested to help you establish what you know and provide a basis for you to develop your knowledge. These plans are designed to provide active learning and involvement but, if you wish, the text may be read independently of them.

We are all managers. We all manage ourselves and our relationships with others, at home, work, school, college and clubs. Managers and supervisors have to do this as part of the job and have specific responsibilities for other people, although they often don't think of management this way. Our hope is that this book will help you manage with people.

Research conducted by Robin Evenden has suggested that most managers are T-types. Their approach shows a technical, thing and task bias and they tackle their job mainly in terms of the function rather than the people managed.

This T-type bias is not surprising. They are likely to have been recruited, trained, coached and rewarded by fellow T-types. Promotion into management is often on the basis of who is good at doing the job rather than who will be able to manage those who are doing it. Those who are good at it usually enjoy it and are reluctant to stop when they become managers. Often no guidance is given in the role of the manager so that in the uncertainty and ambiguity of the new position the only pointer is a technical or professional background. In addition, many business and professional studies courses reinforce this T-type orientation with heavy emphasis upon specialist disciplines and functions such as finance, data processing and marketing.

1

Paradoxically, management job specifications are increasingly being defined in terms of knowledge and skill in managing with people. One of the most frequent criticisms of junior management by their more senior colleagues is that they don't work hard enough at their relationships with others. Perhaps not surprisingly this is the most frequent criticism levelled against more senior management by their subordinates. Management appraisals with great frequency and regularity produce problems related to low concern for people; lack of confidence with others; conflict, communication and relationships difficulties.

There is often a gap between what managers think they ought to be and what they actually are. The next chapter will examine the question in detail, providing opportunities for self assessment of orientation and management style. Before that there are some basic concepts that need to be explored. You may wish to look at the following activity plan.

Activity plan 1

We all manage our relationships with others, and have or may come to have *management* responsibility for subordinates.

We all, in some senses, exercise *authority* in relation to others.

We all work or study within an *organization*, which is one context of our people relationships.

Management, authority and organization are three basic concepts about which we all have some understanding. It is suggested that you examine your own understanding of them by looking at the three questions below.

1 What is management? What is it and what does it do? It may help you to think about yourself as a manager or, if you are being managed, about what your manager does.
2 What is authority? What determines the amount of authority a person has? It may help you to think about the last time somebody made a decision which affected you. How did you respond and what did authority have to do with it? Think of the last time you influenced somebody. What was the basis of your influence?
3 What is an organization? What are its main features? It may help if you think about an organization you know well.

What is management?

A broad definition of management in terms of its purpose is *the efficient and effective use of resources to achieve objectives*. The way that 'use' and 'objectives' are decided depends upon management style, which we shall examine in chapter 2. The 'resources' at management's disposal are the five Ms: money, materials, machines, markets and men.

Another way of looking at management is to describe what it does. Functions frequently identified are:

Policy	deciding what to do and what to aim for
Planning	establishing how to achieve the aims
Organizing	making the arrangements necessary for achievement
Co-ordinating	getting the parts working together
Control	seeing how well the operation is doing and identifying modifications needed.

In the early days of management theory, a common description of the man management function was 'command'. In recent years this has been seen to have overtones of authoritarianism, and other titles such as 'leadership' and 'motivation' are thought to be more appropriate. What they all have in common is the end product, which is to ensure that people in the organization produce results. Another common definition of management is *achieving results with and through other people*. This suggests that the main aim should be to focus on the people who in turn will use other resources to get the results.

Another view of the role of management is that it is there to solve problems.

Problem solving in management

Perhaps if there were no problems there would be no managers. Certainly they have to tackle them. The solution cycle begins with awareness that there is a problem. Events, circumstances or behaviour may be so dramatic that the manager could not avoid being aware of the difficulties. Others may be less easy to detect. Perhaps a decline in morale and performance or an increase in absenteeism has been very gradual, or the boss himself is so much a part of the problem that he fails to recognize that it exists. A related factor is that the manager may exclude himself as a contributory cause of a problem, so that an attempted diagnosis and solution would be incomplete and less effective.

Once awareness exists, the manager begins to seek information which will help problem definition. This means looking at the way it is revealing itself and putting it in a mental pigeon hole of problems. For example, is it a sales, customer relations, administration or personnel problem? When we do this, we should be prepared to accept that our initial pigeon hole may be wrong and

3

Figure 1
Framework: human aspects checklist and action plan

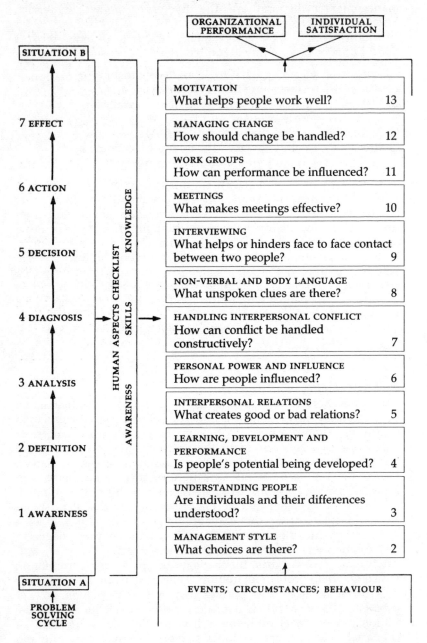

ORGANIZATIONAL PERFORMANCE   INDIVIDUAL SATISFACTION

SITUATION B

MOTIVATION
What helps people work well? 13

7 EFFECT

MANAGING CHANGE
How should change be handled? 12

WORK GROUPS
How can performance be influenced? 11

6 ACTION

MEETINGS
What makes meetings effective? 10

INTERVIEWING
What helps or hinders face to face contact between two people? 9

5 DECISION

NON-VERBAL AND BODY LANGUAGE
What unspoken clues are there? 8

4 DIAGNOSIS

HANDLING INTERPERSONAL CONFLICT
How can conflict be handled constructively? 7

PERSONAL POWER AND INFLUENCE
How are people influenced? 6

3 ANALYSIS

INTERPERSONAL RELATIONS
What creates good or bad relations? 5

LEARNING, DEVELOPMENT AND PERFORMANCE
Is people's potential being developed? 4

2 DEFINITION

UNDERSTANDING PEOPLE
Are individuals and their differences understood? 3

1 AWARENESS

MANAGEMENT STYLE
What choices are there? 2

HUMAN ASPECTS CHECKLIST — KNOWLEDGE — SKILLS — AWARENESS

SITUATION A

EVENTS; CIRCUMSTANCES; BEHAVIOUR

PROBLEM SOLVING CYCLE

4

that we may have to redefine the problem, even perhaps inventing new pigeon holes.

The next stages are analysis and diagnosis, which means identifying the key aspects and then establishing the causes. Analysis breaks down the problem into its component parts, and the diagnosis means seeing the relationship between them. This is the meat of the problem solving process but at the same time it is the most difficult. Paradoxically, these are also the parts often skimped by managers but this may not matter if the problem is familiar and the solution well tried and tested. It is obvious that a wrong diagnosis could result in harmful prescription. Ask any medical practitioner. Thinking is as much part of management as decision making and acting.

An understanding of the causes will provide an indication of the range of solutions, and give a reasoned basis for decision and action, which should have the effect of changing the situation in a positive way.

In reality, problems of different magnitudes are constantly awaiting the manager, and the problem solving cycle is a continuous process. The framework in figure 1 opposite is a human aspects problem solving model as well as being an outline of the structure of this book. It includes the steps in the problem solving cycle but in addition suggests a check-list of factors that need to be taken into account. Each factor is covered by a chapter. The extent of our awareness, skills and knowledge in these human aspects is a major factor in our success in managing with people.

Activity plan 2
Think of a problem that you know about involving people. Work your way through the problem solving cycle using the human aspects checklist (*see* figure 1 opposite). What part does each factor play in the problem? The problem will be a useful case to keep in mind and refer to when you read each chapter of the book. An outline illustration of the framework application follows.

Outline case illustration of framework application as a thinking tool

Awareness: you notice an increase in customer complaints
Definition: sales problem; orders are being lost

Initial analysis	Initial diagnosis	Initial decision/ Initial action
decision delay causes slow response to customer queries	antagonism between two key people who lead sections required to work together; conflict has replaced cooperation and the sections withhold information from each other	you call both section heads and reprimand them, instructing them to work together

Initial effect: the problem increases and the sections find more subtle ways of sabotaging each other's efforts
Redefinition: the situation is now seen as a human aspects problem leading to a decline in sales performance

Analysis factor	Diagnosis	Decision/Action
Management style	you consider your style has been too close to 'abdication' and too 'thing centred'	to assess your style more often and to monitor people and performance more closely
Understanding people	you feel you don't know enough about their personal needs	to get to know their needs and to understand the way they see things
Learning and development	you have not helped them learn the personal and team skills they require	to find out how they learn and to coach them after producing joint action plans; to consider training
Interpersonal relations	negative between the other two, but also a low level of adult transactions between the three of you	to improve positive aspects of relations at an adult level; to be aware of your own impact
Personal influence	negative power and aggression are used	to try assertive techniques
Interpersonal conflict	competition and avoidance are common	to encourage a collaborative mode

Analysis factor	Diagnosis	Decision/Action
Non-verbal behaviour	provided initial clues to the problem but not followed up	to continue to check out non-verbal messages
Interviewing	1 your one to one contact is not frequent enough 2 your interviewing style is inappropriate	to see the individuals more often to try a less direct style in this case
Meetings	your timing of a meeting between the sections added to the social and emotional negative climate and probably increased mutual hostility	to prepare future intersection meetings more thoroughly; attempt some prior defusing and more appropriate timing
Work groups	section heads influence group norms regarding other groups; a win-lose relationship predominates	to work on the section heads' needs and attitudes; check your own relations with the groups; discuss the performance gap; work on the section heads' relations with each other and encourage an intergroup win-win relationship
Managing change	you did not anticipate the impact of an organizational change upon the relations and attitudes of those affected	to consider further reorganization taking into account the concept of socio-technical systems, perhaps using a style in the consultative mode
Motivation	the two section heads now perceive they are competing for scarce rewards of promotion, power, status and job satisfaction as a result of the first organizational change; this was the initial cause of the problem	to clarify the reward structure; appraise, counsel and if possible reassure about rewards

In reality, people and relationships don't fall into neat boxes and the approach illustrated above is not intended to suggest this. All the factors, decisions and actions interact with each other and form a complex process. The point is that the process can be understood better by thinking about its significant elements in a systematic way. The check-list suggests the elements to take into account when faced with problems in the human aspects of management.

Authority in management

The exercise of authority is one of the agents which make organizations live, adapt and survive. It is the influence which is brought to bear upon people, things and decisions and it has several different bases.

Structural authority

Structural authority is the traditional power of the 'boss'. It does not stem from a person nor depend upon personality but is vested in the position that an individual holds within the organization structure. It relates for example to the armed forces, where it is the rank which has to be obeyed and not the person who holds it.

The position at the top has most authority but the source depends upon the nature of the organization. In limited companies authority stems from the shareholders; in public bodies it is derived from statute; in trade unions it is passed on from the members. Authority is the delegated right to make decisions and without this the manager would have no formal powers. The reverse relationship is accountability. The manager has to answer to his boss for the way he uses his delegated authority.

The nature of the right to authority, or what makes it legitimate, is a vexed question. For example, should the source of the right

Structural authority is the traditional power of the 'boss'.

to structural authority in private companies rest solely upon ownership? Or should it be based upon membership of the organization? These are a mixture of political, legal and social issues, and are the root of concepts like participation and employee involvement.

Power is the intervening variable between structural authority and influence upon people and things (*see* figure 2 on page 10). The reality is that power and influence have many different forms and reside in many different parts of an organization. The boss who relies only upon his structural authority is likely to find that his results are affected by conflict and low cooperation.

Expert authority
Expert authority is influence derived from what is known rather than the position held. It is the concept of a person being 'an authority' on a particular subject.

It is vital for management to recognize this form of authority, especially in fields where knowledge is developing rapidly. Indeed, in many organizations expertise will be inversely related to position in the hierarchy. That is to say the higher you are the less you know about specialist areas. The boss cannot be expected to know everything but he needs to know who does know. It is important to consider the implication this has for management decision making style and this will be examined in the next chapter.

Personal authority
Personal authority is the influence an individual has, based upon personal qualities as perceived by other people. It is independent of both position and expertise, and is exercised by people who are not necessarily in management or supervisory positions. This kind of authority links very closely with ideas of leadership and is looked at in chapter 11 on Work Groups.

It is wrong to believe that there is one particular type of leadership personality. There is a popular stereotype of the thrusting extrovert as the ideal leader, but evidence and experience suggests that in many management situations a very different type of person will be influential.

Moral authority
Moral authority is the influence an individual has, based upon moral qualities as perceived by other people. This has nothing to do with wider notions of morality but is essentially related to fairness and impartiality.

9

An individual can claim authority based upon his position: 'Do this because I am the boss'. He can demonstrate authority based upon his expertise: 'Do this because you know I know.' Both these factors, through power or respect, result in influence over people, things and decisions. The other two bases of authority do not operate in quite the same way. It doesn't really work to claim personal authority: 'Do this because I am a great personality'. Nor does it work to assert moral authority: 'Do this because I am telling you that I am fair and impartial.' These two sources of respect and influence have to be ascribed to an individual by other people, including subordinates. They depend entirely upon how that person is perceived and experienced by others. In this sense, the authority of a manager is partly determined by those beneath him.

In conclusion, people in organizations exercise authority based upon the various forms indicated in figure 2 below. Not all these people are managers but a manager's effectiveness depends upon what he is (position); what he knows (expertise); and how he is seen by others (personal and moral). It is very unlikely that the

Figure 2
Different forms of authority in organizations

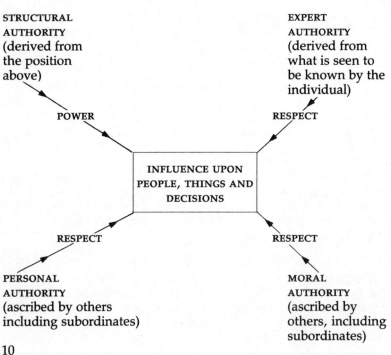

STRUCTURAL
AUTHORITY
(derived from
the position
above)

EXPERT
AUTHORITY
(derived from
what is seen to
be known by the
individual)

POWER

RESPECT

INFLUENCE UPON
PEOPLE, THINGS AND
DECISIONS

RESPECT

RESPECT

PERSONAL
AUTHORITY
(ascribed by others
including subordinates)

MORAL
AUTHORITY
(ascribed by
others, including
subordinates)

10

power of his position, structural authority, will be sufficient as a means of influence with people. Indeed, over-reliance upon this is likely to be counterproductive.

Organizations

Elements common to all organizations

It is important to remember that an organization is made from people, who are individual members with their own personal needs from membership. Individuals will also be members of different kinds of groups. They will belong to work groups, which exist to perform tasks, and social groups which exist to meet individual needs such as friendship. In addition, they may belong to occupational groups (eg engineers, draughtsmen, salesmen); skill and status groups (eg skilled, semi-skilled, white collar) or trade union and staff association groups which represent their interests in various ways. All individuals and work groups have roles to perform within the work organization. A role is the part they are expected to play.

As we have seen earlier, management is a feature of all organizations, and there will be a hierarchy with different levels of structural authority as well as other forms of authority. There will also be goals or objectives. That is, things that the people, groups and organizations as a whole are trying to achieve. Again, there will be both personal goals and organizational goals.

The parts of an organization indicated above are linked together through communication. A network of channels will exist along which messages will be passed, contacts made and relationships formed.

How organizations differ

Shape

Organizational shapes can vary greatly. The number of levels in the hierarchy is a difference, which partly depends upon the scale of operations. There is an obvious difference, for example, between a corner shop's proprietor with one assistant and a large department store with several levels from the shop floor to managing director.

Another factor affecting shape is the span of control of managers and supervisors. This refers to the number of people reporting directly to one person. There was once the myth of the magical seven, which stated dogmatically that any boss should never have more than seven subordinates, because that is the greatest number of people he could watch simultaneously around a meeting table. In recent years research has shown that there is no ideal organizational

11

shape. The number of levels, spans of control and ratio of managers and supervisors to other personnel vary as a result of many factors. One of the most significant is the technical complexity of an organization's operational system. Technical complexity is the extent to which things rather than people perform tasks and exercise control.

Technical complexity increases, for example, in manufacturing industry when the production system moves from unit production to mass production; or from mass production to continuous flow process production. Figures 3, 4 and 5, on pages 13–15, derived from research by Joan Woodward, show how organizational shape varies significantly from one system to another.

Unit production involves making one item at a time, such as an aeroplane. Mass production systems turn out thousands of identical items from assembly lines, such as cars. Continuous flow processes are systems which do not produce separate items, but continuous quantities of a product, such as electricity or refined oil.

Structure
Organizations also differ in their structure. This can usefully be described by the concepts of mechanical and organic organizational structures.

Mechanical	*Organic*
1 The organization is a three sided pyramid consisting of power (structural authority); technical expertise; knowledge of circumstances. With every step down, there is less of all three	Technical expertise is not proportionate with position in the hierarchy. It is important for all levels to have a wide knowledge of the total circumstances of the firm
2 Roles and tasks are clearly defined. Every person knows where the limits of his activity end, and another person's start	Roles and tasks are not clearly defined. The boundary limits between roles are fluid
3 Communication networks are rigid and permanent. Contacts are mainly vertical (ie superior/subordinate)	Communication networks are flexible and transitory. Contacts are frequent outside of the vertical (ie lateral; multi-directional)

Figure 3
The number of levels of authority in management hierarchy

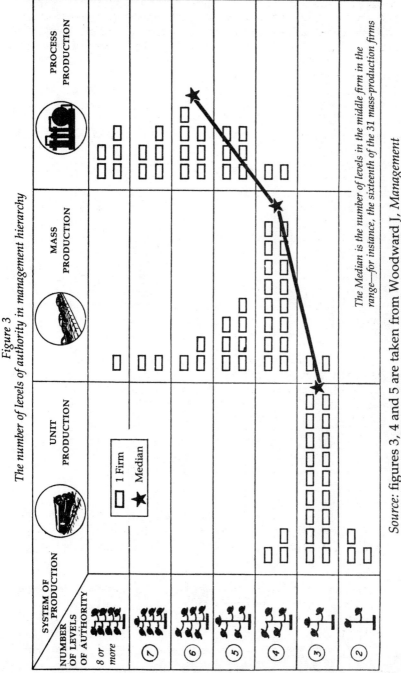

Source: figures 3, 4 and 5 are taken from Woodward J, Management and Technology, HMSO, 1968, reproduced with permission

13

Figure 4
Span of control of first line supervision

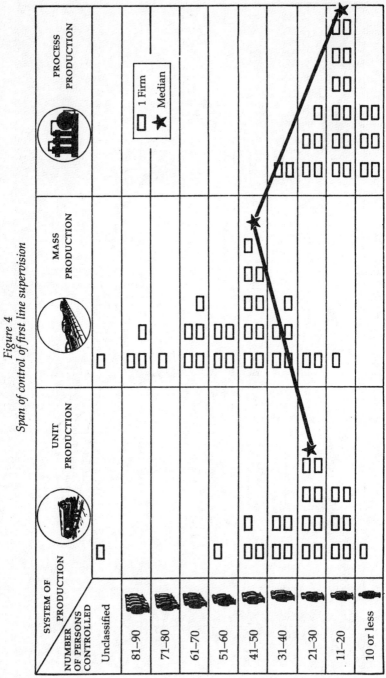

Figure 5

The ratio of managers and supervisory staff to other personnel

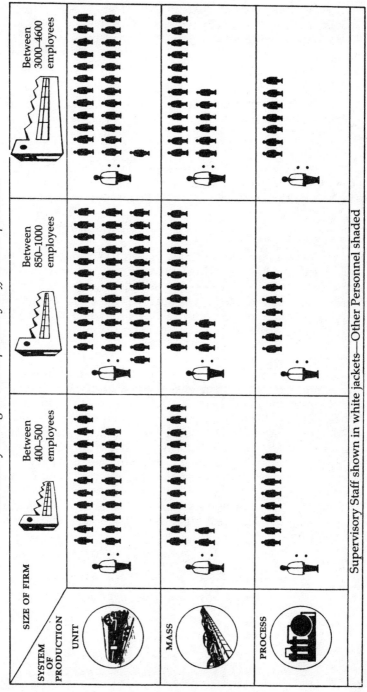

4 Meetings are formal; usually with permanent membership; comparatively infrequent	Meetings are informal; membership fluctuates and consists of varied levels and functions; comparatively frequent
5 The media of communication is mainly written (eg memos)	The media of communication is largely the spoken word
6 Decision making is 'directive' (ie based on structural authority; instructions passed down)	Decision making is 'participant' (ie based on expert authority; frequently consultation between levels and functions)

Organizational research indicates that the mechanical structure is best suited to situations which are static, in the sense that precedents exist for problem solving and decision making and the environment is predictable. On the other hand, the organic structure copes better with situations which are dynamic, when precedents do not exist and the environment is turbulent.

Conflict
Organizations have varying levels of conflict between their parts, and certainly the way managers see conflict can differ dramatically from one organization to another. An interesting distinction here is between organizations as unitary and pluralistic systems. The unitary view, for some the ideal form, is that organizations are essentially happy ships, with harmony the norm and organizational and personal goals in alignment. In the pluralistic system, which is seen by many managers as a more accurate view of reality, organizations are made up of different interests, at times almost like warring tribes, where individuals and groups are in conflict for scarce resources. Most organizations are likely to be at some point between the two poles.

Unitary system	*Pluralistic system*
1 The organization is a team of individuals with common interests and unified by a common purpose	The organization is a coalition of different and divergent interests. There is probably only a limited degree of common purpose, perhaps the only bond being the common interest in the survival of the enterprise
2 There is only one focus of loyalty, and that is allegiance to 'the firm'. Managers have the duty to inspire loyalty, and workers have the obligation to be loyal	There are many rival sources of loyalty, and an individual's prime allegiance is unlikely to be 'the firm'
3 Management has to create a true sense of partnership; a 'happy family'	Management has to accommodate conflicting interests. Conflict can be reduced but not eliminated
4 The level of conflict depends mainly on the quality of personal relationships. Conflict is caused either by 'fools or knaves' or management lacking social skills	The level of conflict depends mainly on factors in the situation, which are 'outside' personal relationships. The trouble-maker explanation is usually a small, if any, part of the truth
5 Conflict is always harmful to the organization	Conflict can sometimes be beneficial to the organization

In conclusion, an organization can be defined as *a collection of individuals, groups, roles and other elements systematically related to each other to achieve results that individuals could not reach so well in isolation.* Organizations differ from each other in terms of shape, structure and conflict. An organization may contain many of these differences within itself. It will change in response to circumstances, so that the modern manager needs to be flexible and aware of the range of managerial choices that can be made. Some of these will be explored in the next chapter.

2 Management style: what kind of boss?

The first section of this chapter is a short introductory text which defines management style. This is followed by section two, the activity plan, which will enable readers to identify their approach to the management of others by the completion of self-assessment exercises and questionnaires. Section three is the concluding text, which identifies factors to consider when assessing the appropriateness of different management styles.

What is management style?

Management style describes the pattern of behaviour which a manager or supervisor uses in relationships with others, particularly subordinates or those more junior in status. It is concerned with the way authority and leadership is exercised by the manager and the response that comes from other people. It is the essence of management and relates to all its functions.

Style is about behaviour. It is about what managers *do* rather than what they *are*. This point is important because it indicates that styles can be observed, described and therefore become known to the individual concerned. It also suggests that the manager can become aware of a range of alternative styles, or behaviour patterns, and can within limits make choices about which is most appropriate to the situation being managed.

Undoubtedly management style is a key factor in the success of the manager, organization, department or section. It is a vital part of achieving results through others.

Three dimensions of management style

There are three important aspects of a manager's style in relationship to other people. First, communication style: how decisions are made and solutions found. Secondly, the proportion of time devoted to the technical aspects of the job as opposed to people. Thirdly, the social relationship with subordinates or those junior in status.

Each of these three dimensions will be described; it is emphasized that the intention is not to label different styles as 'good' or 'bad' in themselves but simply to identify their respective characteristics in a recognizable way.

It also needs emphasizing that an individual is unlikely to be managing from one fixed point; a style describes an average or 'most frequent' mode of behaviour. In practice, a manager is likely to range either side of the point on the style dimension scales.

1 Communication style: problem solving/decision making
The first dimension describes the different ways that a manager can relate to subordinates or juniors in decision making or problem solving. It shows that the manager can choose different degrees of sharing authority and influence with others, and that the choice affects the degree of involvement and initiative that subordinates can have. (*See* figure 6 on page 20.)

There are three major style modes: directive, consultative and participant, and the behaviour ranges from 'telling' through to 'delegating'.

2 Priorities style: things or people
Style can be described in terms of the time spent on 'technical' (thing) matters compared with that spent on 'people' matters. Very often a manager will place an emphasis upon one aspect or the other, and the most frequent bias is towards the 'technical' or thing end of the dimension scale. This is called T-type management, and the bias may result from the demands of the job but usually stems from the manager's interest, indeed success, in the technical aspects of his function, which results in his promotion. Of course, when he is promoted, the new role may require more emphasis on people and less on technical aspects, which subordinates may be employed to look after. Some managers find it difficult to take off their technical 'blinkers' when they are promoted to management and this will create problems.

It is possible to analyse the way a manager spends his time at work according to estimates of the technical/people content of his activities, and the time spent on them (*see* figure 7 on page 21). Some activities will be one or the other but quite often there will be a mix of both technical and people focus within an activity.

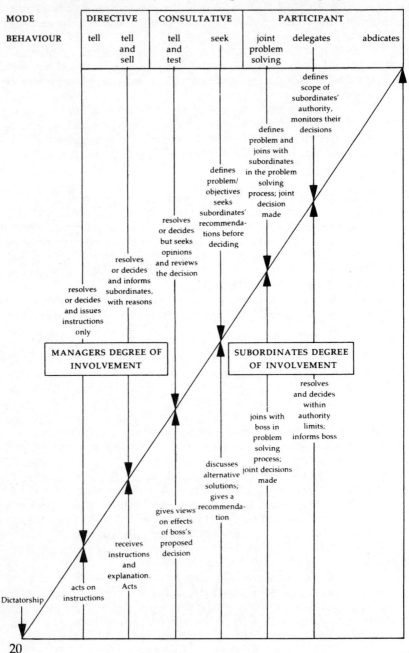

Figure 6
Communication: problem solving/decision making style

MODE: DIRECTIVE | CONSULTATIVE | PARTICIPANT

BEHAVIOUR: tell | tell and sell | tell and test | seek | joint problem solving | delegates | abdicates

defines scope of subordinates' authority, monitors their decisions

defines problem and joins with subordinates in the problem solving process; joint decision made

defines problem/ objectives seeks subordinates' recommendations before deciding

resolves or decides but seeks opinions and reviews the decision

resolves or decides and informs subordinates, with reasons

resolves or decides and issues instructions only

MANAGERS DEGREE OF INVOLVEMENT

SUBORDINATES DEGREE OF INVOLVEMENT

resolves and decides within authority limits; informs boss

joins with boss in problem solving process; joint decisions made

discusses alternative solutions; gives a recommendation

gives views on effects of boss's proposed decision

receives instructions and explanation. Acts

acts on instructions

Dictatorship

20

Figure 7
Priorities style: things or people

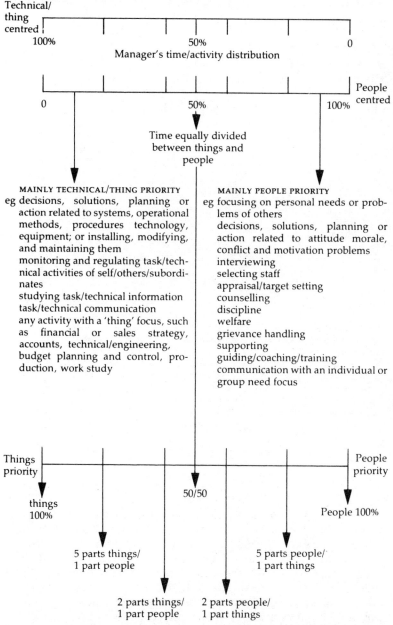

Technical/
thing
centred

100%   50%   0

Manager's time/activity distribution

0   50%   100% People
centred

Time equally divided
between things and
people

MAINLY TECHNICAL/THING PRIORITY
eg decisions, solutions, planning or action related to systems, operational methods, procedures technology, equipment; or installing, modifying, and maintaining them
monitoring and regulating task/technical activities of self/others/subordinates
studying task/technical information
task/technical communication
any activity with a 'thing' focus, such as financial or sales strategy, accounts, technical/engineering, budget planning and control, production, work study

MAINLY PEOPLE PRIORITY
eg focusing on personal needs or problems of others
decisions, solutions, planning or action related to attitude morale, conflict and motivation problems
interviewing
selecting staff
appraisal/target setting
counselling
discipline
welfare
grievance handling
supporting
guiding/coaching/training
communication with an individual or group need focus

Things
priority

things
100%

50/50

People
priority

People 100%

5 parts things/
1 part people

5 parts people/
1 part things

2 parts things/
1 part people

2 parts people/
1 part things

21

It is important to emphasize that both technical centred managers and people centred managers can have equal concern for task accomplishment. Where they differ is the priority style adopted in order to facilitate performance of the manager's section, department or organization.

3 Sociability style

The manager's behaviour related to social relationships with others at work is another important aspect of style. It reflects the extent of his or her sociability (*see* figure 8 below).

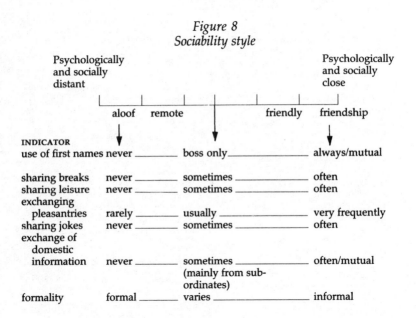

Figure 8
Sociability style

At one extreme, psychologically and socially close, the manager would behave as if he was 'one of the boys or girls', and would attempt to develop friendship links with subordinates. This would involve the sharing of leisure and social activities and other things that the term 'friendship' implies. The 'distant' extreme is manifested by a style which is devoid of any informality in the boss/subordinate relationship. First name terms would be positively prohibited and even conventional civilities would be unusual.

22

There are, of course, intermediate positions and the degree of closeness is indicated by many factors, some of which are indicated in figure 8. For example, how often does the manager share his 'break' times with more junior employees; how frequently are conversational pleasantries exchanged; how much mutual domestic information is exchanged; to what extent do boss and subordinates share jokes and so on?

T-type managers: some managers find it difficult to take off their technical 'blinkers' when they are promoted.

Activity plans

The text has described three dimensions of management style and indicates significant aspects of a manager's relationship with others. Do you know your style? It is worth considering where you are on the style dimensions, and you may find it helps to assess others and be assessed by them. The activity plan will give you an opportunity to do this, and includes a style and leadership questionnaire which may also provide you with interesting information. The assessments should be in relation to subordinates. If you have none, then in relation to others who are 'junior' to you. The activity plans are as follows:

        1 Management style: how you see it
        2 Management style: how others see it
        3 Management style: questionnaire

Remember, Attila the Hun and Mahatma Gandhi were both successful.

1 Management style: how you see it

You will need somebody to assess. Yourself? Your boss? Your wife

23

or husband? Your teacher? Take whatever time scale you wish when making your assessment, but the last two months will not require too great a feat of memory and are probably long enough.

What is your (or your boss's etc) average or most frequent position on the two scales below? It may vary from time to time but guesstimate as best you can, either by casting your mind back over the last few months *or* by observing the style behaviour during the next few days.

Record your assessments on the scales. You may do this in several ways. Perhaps simply with one 'X' on the average or most frequent position, or a more detailed style profile (see below).

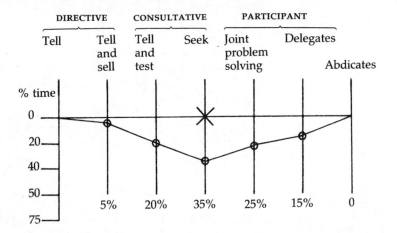

Example
This guesstimate shows that the most frequent style 'X' is assessed as the 'seek' style in the consultative mode. The graph profile represents the frequencies with which an individual displays different styles.

Communication: problem solving/decision making style (Refer to Figure 6)

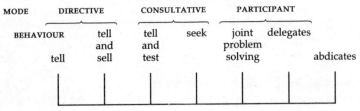

24

Priorities style: things or people (Refer to figure 7)

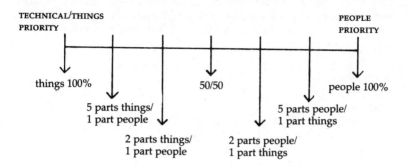

Sociability style

In order to assess this management style dimension, make a rating for your subject (You? Your boss?) on each of the indicators below. Add the scores together, divide by 7 to give you the average and this will be the guesstimate of the sociability style.

INDICATOR	1	2	3	4	5	6	7
use of first names	never •	•	•	boss only uses it •	•	•	always/ mutual •
sharing break times	never •	•	•	sometimes •	•	•	often •
sharing leisure outside work	never •	•	•	sometimes •	•	•	often •
exchanging pleasantries	rarely •	•	•	usually •	•	•	very often •
sharing jokes/ humour	never •	•	•	sometimes •	•	•	often •
exchanging domestic information	never •	•	•	sometimes: mostly from subordinates •	•	•	often/ mutual •
formality	very formal •	•	•	varies •	•	•	very informal •

1	2	3	4	5	6	7
psychologically and socially distant aloof from subordinates			remote	friendly	psychologically and socially close friendship with subordinates	

25

2 Management style: how others see it

How you see yourself is a useful and interesting thing to clarify, and this you may have done using the three dimension scales in activity 1. Is this different from the way others see you?

If you are able, why not get somebody who knows you well (your husband, wife, a close work colleague or, if you dare, even a subordinate) to assess *you* on the three dimensions. That will be interesting and valuable feedback in itself to see yourself as others see you.

If there are differences between your assessment of yourself, and the other person's assessment of you, a discussion of the disparities may be rewarding.

It could be that there is a disparity because you understand the dimensions differently, in which case this may lead to clarification of the concepts of style. On the other hand, the divergence may be a real difference in perceptions and discussion around this may be very rewarding. You will probably find it most beneficial if you simply explore your reasons for the different views, rather than try to convince each other that you are right and the other person is wrong in their assessment.

Another interesting activity is for a pair or small group to compare styles, note the differences and see if you can establish good reasons for the divergence.

Indeed, what *do* you take into account when deciding upon a style? If you have never really thought about it before, think about it now. What *ought* you to take into account? Do this before you read section three, below, which suggests some important factors.

3 Management style: questionnaire

This questionnaire will give you a things/people priorities style rating. It is based upon the way you see yourself in relation to a number of factors which provide clues about management style.

Directions Respond to each item according to the way you would most likely act if you were the leader of a work group. Do not spend long thinking about each item. Circle whether you would most likely behave in the described way: always (A), frequently (F), occasionally (O), seldom (S), or never (N).

1 I would most likely act as the spokesman of the group   A F O S N

2 I would encourage overtime work   A F O S N

3 I would allow members complete freedom in their work   A F O S N

4 I would encourage the use of uniform procedures — A F O S N

5 I would permit the members to use their own judgement in solving problems — A F O S N

6 I would stress being ahead of competing groups — A F O S N

7 I would speak as a representative of the group — A F O S N

8 I would needle members for greater effort — A F O S N

9 I would try out my ideas in the group — A F O S N

10 I would let the members do their work the way they think best — A F O S N

11 I would be working hard for a promotion — A F O S N

12 I would tolerate postponement and uncertainty — A F O S N

13 I would speak for the group if there were visitors present — A F O S N

14 I would keep the work moving at a rapid pace — A F O S N

15 I would turn the members loose on a job and let them go to it — A F O S N

16 I would settle conflicts when they occur in the group — A F O S N

17 I would get swamped by details — A F O S N

18 I would represent the group at outside meetings — A F O S N

19 I would be reluctant to allow the members any freedom of action — A F O S N

20 I would decide what should be done and how it should be done — A F O S N

21 I would push for increased production — A F O S N

22 I would let some members have authority which I could keep — A F O S N

23 Things would usually turn out as I had predicted — A F O S N

24 I would allow the group a high degree of initiative — A F O S N

25 I would assign group members to particular tasks — A F O S N

26 I would be willing to make changes — A F O S N

27 I would ask the members to work harder — A F O S N

28 I would trust the group members to exercise good judgement — A F O S N

29 I would schedule the work to be done — A F O S N

30 I would refuse to explain my actions — A F O S N

31 I would persuade others that my ideas are to their advantage — A F O S N

32 I would permit the group to set its own pace — A F O S N

33 I would urge the group to beat its previous record — A F O S N

34 I would act without consulting the group — A F O S N

35 I would ask that group members follow standard rules and regulations — A F O S N

P ——————————————— T ———————————

Source: J W Pfeiffer and J E Jones, *A Handbook of Structured Experiences*, University Associates, 1974.

The management style—scoring questionnaire

1 Circle the item number for items 8, 12, 17, 18, 19, 30, 34 and 35 (ie the actual number 8, 12 etc. Thus ⑧ . . .).

2 Write the number 1 in front of a *circled item number* if you responded S (seldom) or N (never) to that item.

3 Also write a number 1 in front of *item numbers not circled* if you responded A (always) or F (frequently).

4 Circle the number 1s which you have written in front of the following items: 3, 5, 8, 10, 15, 18, 19, 22, 24, 26, 28, 30, 32, 34 and 35.

5 *Count the circled number 1s.* This is the score for concern for people. Record the score in the blank following the letter P at the end of the questionnaire.

6 *Count the uncircled number 1s.* This is the score for concern for task. Record this number in the blank following the letter T.

7 Record your T and P scores on the scale dimension below.

8 Divide in half the length between your T and P scores (ie mark the mid-point). This will be the questionnaire's indication of your thing/people priority style.

Management styles: people—thing priorities

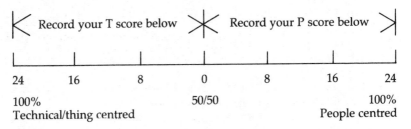

Compare your score with the other ratings on priorities style in activities 1 and 2. If they are close to each other, this is reinforcement of the assessment. It is sometimes the case that the questionnaire produces results different from earlier assessments. There are sometimes differences between the way we would like to be, think we ought to be and the way we are. Do the variations in your assessments give you food for thought?

It must be emphasized that the questionnaire is based on studies of management style but it is not a scientific instrument which produces a 'true' answer. It is best to see such questionnaires as facilitators of thought and discussion rather than a revelation of the truth.

In any event, it is vital for a manager periodically to ask himself informed questions about his management style and to have a clear idea about how to describe it. Judgement then has to be made whether or not the style is appropriate in the circumstances of the manager. Factors to take into account will be considered in the section which follows.

The contingency theory of management style

Is there a 'best' position on the three dimensions of style that all managers should aspire towards? No doubt some theorists and managers claim that there is, largely on the basis of their own values and what they feel 'ought' to be the case. But there is a great deal of apparently contradictory evidence. For example, some studies show that a directive/thing centred style produces the best performance results. Others demonstrate just the opposite, that a participant/people centred style has a better effect.

An increasing body of research and management opinion is now suggesting that these divergent results can be reconciled by the so called 'contingency' theory. This indicates that there is not a single best management style, but only styles that are more or less appropriate depending upon a variety of factors in the situation and the criteria for measuring success. This implies that if key factors change, the style needs to change to match it.

Choosing and using the appropriate style is still more of an art than a science. Nevertheless, it can be an art based upon informed and reasoned judgements which take into account factors that experience and experiment suggest are significant.

Factors affecting the appropriateness of styles

Yourself: natural style

It can be argued that people have 'natural' styles of management. Certainly many managers find themselves comfortable with some styles and uncomfortable with others. To adopt a style without subscribing to the values associated with it, or to play a part which is out of character will soon be detected as false and will be difficult to sustain. The results are likely to be counterproductive.

This is not to imply that a manager's repertoire is narrow. Most people are able to play tunes over a wide range of the three style scales and are able to exercise a degree of choice in monitoring and modifying their own behaviour. This is known as style flex.

For example, a shy manager would have problems in playing one of the boys, although he may well move from the aloof end of the sociability scale by exchanging pleasantries more frequently, becoming less formal and perhaps sharing humour. Over time he may find these experiments in style rewarding and the so-called natural limits may be gradually extended.

29

The newly promoted manager

Selecting an appropriate sociability style can be difficult for the newly promoted manager or supervisor, especially when they remain in the same department. Often it is better to choose a safe mid-scale position for the first few months, with a gradual transition to the style which emerges as appropriate.

If the new manager adopts a psychologically close one of the boys style, he may be seen by his fellow managers or supervisors as identifying more with his subordinates than with them. On the other hand, a move to the other extreme may be seen by previous colleagues as an unpleasant change of allegiance and relations with them would become difficult. It is a situation requiring skill and sensitivity, to avoid getting off to a bad start. To be effective, the man in the middle must realize that he is in the middle and must relate effectively in both directions, thus acting as a link pin between levels.

Subordinates: personality, expertise and expectations

The personality of subordinates and characteristics of work groups have a bearing on style appropriateness. For example, research evidence has shown that individuals and groups operating in an independent fashion do not respond well to a style which is psychologically close. Some individuals may feel that such a style infringes their 'psychological space' or privacy.

Individuals having a high need for security may welcome a more directive decision making style which relieves them of the anxieties of responsibility. Others may want a more participant, delegating approach to meet their needs for self-esteem and fulfilment.

The manager should also be objective about the distribution of expertise in his area of responsibility. In many organizations technical expertise and knowledge of specific circumstances will increase at lower levels and decrease at higher levels. If this is so, the boss will need to use subordinates' know-how in order to achieve effective decisions, either by a consultative or participant style mode. Should the boss be the expert, his options are different and may require a more directive approach, although this may be tempered by the need to have the commitment of subordinates to solutions and decisions.

Subordinates are likely to have developed expectations about the style of their boss, particularly if they have worked together for a long time. Sudden and dramatic changes, perhaps after reading a book or attending a course, have sometimes been known to have disastrous results on relationships. This does not mean that there is a requirement from subordinates that their boss should not use style flex, or adapt the approach to circumstances, but that

30

this happens in a way which they can reasonably anticipate and understand.

Pressures to conform from boss and colleagues
It is common for organizations to have a 'house style' and an individual who breaks the rules can be subjected to all the pressures placed upon non-conformers in groups. Often these are subtle hints and implicit norms but the new manager will rapidly learn the expectations of bosses and colleagues. Styles and ways of doing things are often built into the customs of organizations and become part of its fabric. This means that individuals can be constrained by these factors and can place limitations upon their style flex.

Some organizations are now examining their culture and customs, and are attempting to build different relationships between individuals and groups as well as trying to modify management 'house-styles'. This has come to be known as organization development.

Some organizations permit boss and subordinate to choose complementary styles. Thus a manager and a deputy manager between them can cover a wide range of the style dimensions. For example, a T-type technical centred and distant boss may be supported by a second in command who looks after the people side of the operation, or vice versa.

The nature of the job and situation
Some managers are constrained by their function and special skills to adopt a particular style. For example, a manager who is a qualified accountant in charge of a department often has a job which demands frequent use of technical expertise and will focus on this more than people. However, this is sometimes due to the way he or she chooses to interpret the role, based on what he likes doing and is good at. It may not always be the emphasis which is appropriate for the achievement of departmental objectives.

There are other key situational factors to take into account when attempting to make an objective view of your style and its situational fit (*see* figure 9 on page 32). For example, choice of communication style should in part be based upon your assessment of where your organization or department is on the 'stability/ dynamism' continuum. If it is operating in a stable situation, where previous decisions may simply have to be reproduced, then a more directive style may be best. When there is a dynamic situation, where events and problems are often unprecedented, a more participant style may be called for.

Figure 9
Situational factors and indicators management style fit

	DIRECTIVE/CONSULTATIVE MODE	PARTICIPANT/CONSULTATIVE MODE
TASKS	routine/simple	non-routine/complex
PROBLEMS	predictable/precedented	unpredictable/unprecedented
NEED FOR JUDGEMENT	low	high
ENVIRONMENT	stable/static	change/dynamic
TASK/PROBLEM RELATED EXPERTISE	mainly with boss	mainly with subordinates
PERIODIC PRESSURE	high	low
CREATIVITY REQUIRED	low	high
DECISION URGENCY	high	low
PEOPLE PROBLEMS	infrequent/slight	frequent/severe
SUBORDINATES PERSONAL GOALS	security/social	achievement/involvement

	DIRECTIVE STYLE OUTCOMES	PARTICIPANT STYLE OUTCOMES
TASK	limits time spent communicating reduces chance of subordinates making mistakes good decisions/solutions if boss *is* the expert	clarification through mutual feedback provides control and monitoring information several minds contribute to decision/solution
INDIVIDUAL AND GROUP	Provides a secure and undemanding environment	assists the identification and diagnosis of attitude, morale and motivation problem individuals have opportunity for involvement, achievement and recognition group opportunity for social rewards through collaboration

32

Similarly, the nature of subordinates' jobs, and their level of skill and scope for initiative are factors to take into account. Pressures and urgency are further factors which should be considered as a determinant of style.

Figure 10
Peak period pressure and management style

High pressure	Participant: people priority	Directive: things priority
Low pressure	Directive: things priority	Participant: people priority
	Low performance	High performance

Research suggests that peak period pressures should be associated with style flex (see figure 10 above). The study looked at retail, with pronounced selling peaks at week-ends, and food processing, with production peaks at harvest time. When the pressure was on it was the directive and things priority styles which were more likely to be associated with high performing groups. The reverse tended to be true when pressure was off the group. This was strong support for the style flex concept, because the managers who modified their approach appropriately according to the pressure peaks and troughs were most likely to be associated with high performing groups. Those who were 'inflexible' tended to have lower performance from their groups. A key factor though was that the group understood the reasons for the change in style.

Leadership goals and management style
The ideas of style flex and contingency theory support the view that there is not one best style that managers should aspire towards.

The conclusion is that managers must play tunes upon the style dimension scales according to their interpretation of the situation scores.

It has been argued that, although styles may vary, all managers of people have three functions to perform or goals to achieve. These are concerned with the task, group and individuals (*see* figure 11 on page 35). All three are interrelated and the manager's job is to use a style which maintains an optimum balance between

Figure 11
Leadership goals

There are three goals of leadership, each affecting and being affected by the others.

TASK GOALS	1. Achieving the best solutions or decisions 2. Ensuring that groups or individuals accomplish their tasks in the most effective way
INDIVIDUAL GOALS	1. Helping individuals to meet their needs/goals 2. Avoiding individual frustrations 3. Maintaining an individual's involvement 4. Helping the individual to gain satisfaction from the activity and its outcome
GROUP GOALS	1. Ensuring that individuals collaborate well as a group; team building 2. Containing unproductive conflict 3. Managing tensions within the group so that it does not disintegrate

them. The need is to place the right relative emphasis upon each goal or activity so that the 'whole' style is appropriate to the situation being managed.

The message of this chapter has been that managers need to monitor themselves and their styles, and to bring the three dimensional relationship with others into the area of conscious choice and judgement. In all situations the manager is concerned with relationships with others both as individuals and members of groups. These areas, of vital concern for the manager, will be explored in subsequent chapters.

3 Understanding people

This chapter looks at different ways of understanding people in terms of attitudes, perception and personality. Some dangers are looked at and some approaches suggested which may help us understand the complexity of people at work.

The primary unit of any organization, large or small, and of departments within it, is the individual. If a manager knows what factors influence an individual's behaviour, including his own, he is better able to manage effectively. To understand behaviour it is also necessary to consider attitudes, perceptions and personality and the links between these. It must be stressed right away that there is no 'magic formula' for this: people, perhaps fortunately, are far too complex. But some valuable insights can be gained. A useful approach is the analogy of an 'onion' type model, where each layer of 'skin' is peeled to reveal another underneath. The outside layer represents behaviour, what is said, done, written, etc, the manifestation of 'what lies within the onion'.

One of the best-known studies of behaviour was that carried out by Pavlov on dogs. He gave food to the dogs and found that they salivated. In the next stage he gave food and rang a bell, and they salivated. After some time simply ringing the bell without giving food caused the dogs to salivate. Pavlov called this a 'conditioned reflex', ie a stimulus leading directly to a response.

STIMULUS → RESPONSE

Is this too simple a view to take of human behaviour? When the variety of reactions that individuals have to the same situation are considered it is clearly apparent that the same stimulus can result in widely different responses. Some of the reasons for this are differences of attitude, perceptions and personality.

Attitudes

Attitudes are a relatively enduring organization of beliefs around an objective or situation predisposing a person to respond in some preferential manner. That is, they are influences upon how we see and react to things. It is interesting to note that first-hand experience is not required to form a definite set of attitudes; for instance, some people have opinions and attitudes about unions without ever having been a union member. Attitudes are formed from a number of sources. There are those factors such as experience, values and beliefs that tend to be internal to the individual, while others such as norms, loyalties etc. tend to be external and come from a significant person or group of people with whom the individual identifies. Attitudes develop and change through one of the following ways:

Compliance—'or else'

When a manager has power over a subordinate, perhaps due to control of earnings or promotion, the subordinate may comply to the wishes of the boss and appear to adopt an acceptable attitude. This is the 'or else' approach to changing attitudes. Such a change is likely to be superficial, short-term and will disappear when the threat or promise is removed.

Identification—'like me'

If a manager is adopted as a 'rôle model' by a subordinate, attempts will be made to take on the characteristic attitudes of the boss. Values and behaviour may be 'copied'. It is rather like teenagers using pop stars or sportsmen/women as models to follow. This is the 'like me' approach to influencing attitudes. It suggests to subordinates 'like me' and 'be like me'. The subordinate identifies or is invited to identify with the boss. The individual believes in the attitudes and values which will be adopted until a more significant role model appears or the boss is found to have feet of clay.

Internalization—'it's right'

This is where an individual discovers different values and works out that a particular attitude is right. The manager may help, perhaps by counselling, so that subordinates are clear about their attitudes, perhaps re-evaluate them. The individual makes the change on the basis that 'it is right'. When this 'internalization' process occurs the attitude change is likely to be long-lasting.

37

Perceptions

Picture A

Activity plan 1
Look at the picture above for about 10 seconds. Then look at picture B for about 10 seconds, and write down briefly what you see.

Picture B

Activity plan 2

Please read each of these statements made by famous people and indicate whether you tend to agree or disagree with them.

	agree	disagree
1 'Rebellion has been the spur to progress for mankind' (J F Kennedy)	____	____
2 'To be free people must conform to the law of the State' (Stalin)	____	____
3 'It is determination that is the key to making things happen, for ourselves, for our families and for our nation' (Harry Truman)	____	____
4 'The minority must give way to the greater good of the majority, that is what social progress is all about' (Adolf Hitler)	____	____
5 'To make changes is always painful' (Idi Amin)	____	____
6 'Fear is the ghost that sits upon our shoulder; exorcise it and be free' (Winston Churchill)	____	____
7 'History is a great teacher; it teaches us we rarely learn from our mistakes' (Abraham Lincoln)	____	____
8 'Leadership is the art of getting those to be led to believe in what you offer them' (Mussolini)	____	____

It is a characteristic of the human mind that all people, to a greater or lesser extent, can be predisposed in favour of certain conclusions. The simple experiments in Activity 1 and 2 are likely to demonstrate this. People's descriptions of what they see in Picture B usually include the fact that it is a 'young woman' whereas, if they were shown picture C (below) first instead of picture A, they tend to see an 'old woman' in picture B. You might like to try this with your friends.

Picture C

Equally, in Activity 2, none of the statements were made by the people listed: they were simply designed to illustrate that people can be influenced (or predisposed) not only by what is said but who said it. Of the supposed authors, four are generally regarded as 'baddies' and four as 'goodies':

'Baddies'	'Goodies'
Stalin	J F Kennedy
Adolf Hitler	Harry Truman
Idi Amin	Winston Churchill
Mussolini	Abraham Lincoln

By looking at your answers you will be able to see to what extent you have been predisposed. You can experiment further with this by changing the quotes around and trying the activity with others. Of course, not too much should be taken from what after all are two very simple experiments, but nevertheless perceptions are often strongly influenced in real life by things about which we aren't fully aware. For example, people who decide to buy a particular car often find that they notice such models much more frequently than before; their mental 'set' of predispositions has resulted in selective perception. Equally, a characteristic of the 'halo' effect is to heighten sensitivity to what is regarded as 'good' in the other person and reduced perception of the 'bad'; the 'horns' effect is the reverse of this in that the negative things are selectively perceived and the positive largely missed.

One other way in which this occurs is through the tendency of the mind to build up a 'complete' picture even when there is insufficient information to do this, so that such a picture is often not accurate and has to be changed when more information becomes available. Sometimes the information will be altered by selection or filtering so that we don't alter our initial picture. Also, differing people will perceive the same person or situation differently to some extent because everyone interprets from a unique base. In this way, inferences and interpretations involved in perception are affected by the individual's process of filtering, so that our own attitudes, values, experience, feelings etc colour our perceptions.

A consequence is that managers need to be aware of their own predispositions which might lead to self-fulfilling situations. For example, a manager who has a predisposition not to trust his subordinates to get on with the job, and thus controls them very closely, will set up a situation where they behave the way he is predisposed to expect, thus confirming a self-fulfilling prophecy.

One type of predisposition is to do with biases. In any society or culture, there tend to be favourable or unfavourable biases towards other people based upon behaviour characteristics. Often the biases have no substance in fact. In the UK some of the generally favourable biases are to do with neatness, a firm handshake, politeness and conventional clothes; unfavourable ones are often concerned with untidiness, eccentric dress, a weak handshake or chin.

Personality

Beneath attitudes—the next layer of the skin of the onion as it were—are the relatively stable collection of things like motives, needs and values that go to make up personality. Personality can be defined as the blend of innate and acquired traits in the make-up of a person. Thus personality can be seen to arise from the interaction between biological drives and the social and physical environment. This is often referred to as the Nurture v Nature controversy, that is, the extent to which personality is influenced by genetic factors or the social and physical environment. Some psychologists argue that it is primarily influenced by heredity, others that the balance is the other way.

Figure 12
Nature v Nurture

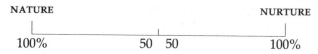

Modern research has revealed that there are at least two axes involved in the dimensions of personality; introversion/extraversion and stable/unstable. An extravert is a person most interested in the external world of objects and people, an introvert a person most interested in his own thoughts and feelings.

The two axes are shown in the model in figure 13 on page 42. Four quadrants, unstable extravert, unstable introvert, stable introvert and stable extravert are shown, and some of the characteristic traits are written around the rim. Modern psychologists prefer trait (descriptions of habitual behaviour patterns) theories to type theories.

The chart shows the relationship of introversion/extraversion and neuroticism/stability. A person could be assigned a position on each of the two axes, ie more or less stable, more or less extraverted. This is the view now widely accepted and the trait names given in the outer circle are the results of a good deal of modern research.

As has been stressed, all combinations of scores on the two continua extraversion–introversion and stable–unstable are possible.

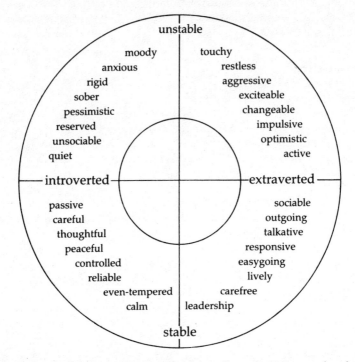

Figure 13
Schemas of personality

unstable

moody   touchy
anxious   restless
rigid   aggressive
sober   exciteable
pessimistic   changeable
reserved   impulsive
unsociable   optimistic
quiet   active

introverted   extraverted

passive   sociable
careful   outgoing
thoughtful   talkative
peaceful   responsive
controlled   easygoing
reliable   lively
even-tempered   carefree
calm   leadership

stable

Source: Eysenck H J, *Fact and Fiction in Psychology*, Penguin, 1965, reproduced with permission

The terms extravert–introvert are used in the sense that there is a continuum from one extreme end to another, with most people occupying their average position nearer the centre than the extremes. Thus it is not correct to think of the two terms as two type or classes, rather as extreme points on a scale, running from 100 per cent extravert to 100 per cent introvert. People are almost never complete extraverts or complete introverts. Most people are ambiverts, sometimes most involved in their environment, sometimes in themselves.

In no sense is the extravert superior or inferior to the introvert; they are just different. The extravert may be sociable, cheerful, always on the go, likes being with people, tells jokes etc, and all this can make him a social asset. On the other hand, he may be unreliable, changes friends frequently, is easily bored and finds it difficult to get on with uninteresting jobs. The introvert tends to be the opposite of all this; from a work point of view he could be greatly preferable unless that work brings him into frequent contact with people.

Some organizations use personality tests as one method of selecting staff, although many of these are in fact trying to measure attitudes, perception and behavioural preferences. It is unlikely that the inner core of the personality can easily be changed, certainly not at the whim of a manager. However, managers frequently need to make judgements about people for many reasons, including selection, development and performance influence.

Tools to help the manager understand people include sophisticated Assessment Centres, which incorporate careful descriptions of what is required from people in a particular job or organization. These centres usually involve the acquisition of a great deal of evidence about individuals, from psychological tests, interviews and group activities designed to reveal attitudes and behaviour preferences. However, for most day to day purposes, the manager has to rely on simpler tools for understanding and assessing people. Often the basis of judgement is the mental frameworks which have been acquired willy nilly over the years. We need to bear in mind the earlier points made about perception when we reflect upon how valid and reliable these frameworks may be.

Activity plan 3
The following questionnaire will help you assess how you think about people at work. From each of the paired statements below, select one which best fits your view.

1.1 People are mainly interested in money at work
 2 The most important thing at work is your colleagues

2.1 People work best if there is a good team spirit
 2 The best motivation is self-motivation

3.1 People like to be left alone to get on with the job
 2 Feelings get in the way of doing a good job

4.1 People calculate their self-interest above all else at work
 2 People need a boss who is easy to get on with

5.1 The most important thing at work is your colleagues
 2 What people want most from work is a chance to use their skills and abilities

6.1 The best motivation is self-motivation
 2 People have to be controlled if they are to work well

7.1 Feelings get in the way of doing a good job
   2 People are more influenced by their colleagues than their boss

8.1 People need a boss who is easy to get on with
   2 An interesting job is the best guarantee of good work

9.1 What people want most from work is a chance to use their skills and abilities
   2 People are mainly interested in money at work

10.1 People have to be controlled if they are to work well
   2 People work best if there is a good team spirit

11.1 People are more influenced by their colleagues than their boss
   2 People like to be left alone to get on with the job

12.1 An interesting job is the best guarantee of good work
   2 People calculate their self-interest above all else at work

Scoring key

The questionnaire consists of statements reflecting each of three common stereotypes of people at work:

   Rational economic stereotype
   Social stereotype
   Self-fulfilment stereotype

Each statement is paired with one statement from each of the other two stereotypes. The key indicates how to score the questionnaire. For example, if you choose the first statement of the first pair you would score one for the Rational economic stereotype. If you chose the second statement in the second pair you would score one for the Self-fulfilment stereotype and so on. The maximum score for any one stereotype is 8 and the total score is 12. A score of more than 4 for any stereotype suggests that you have it as one of your ways of generalizing about people.

Remember that this is not a 'scientific' instrument revealing the 'truth' about you, but only a device to help you and others think about how you see people at work. Use it as one piece of evidence amongst others which may help you reflect upon how you 'understand' people.

Circle the answer you gave for each pair. For example, if you chose statement 2 for question one, circle '2'. When completed for all twelve, add the circles for each of the three columns.

If you scored similarly on all the 'stereotypes' it probably means that you don't hold any of these three general views of people at

44

Statement pair	Rational economic	Social	Self-fulfilment
1	1	2	
2		1	2
3	2		1
4	1	2	
5		1	2
6	2		1
7	1	2	
8		1	2
9	2		1
10	1	2	
11		1	2
12	2		1
TOTALS			

work. On the other hand, if you scored 6 or more on one and 2 or less on another, this could indicate a 'stereotype' which you have.

People stereotypes

We often develop 'stereotypes' or fixed general views about people. These generalizations may actually get in the way of understanding individuals because we see what we expect to see rather than what is really there. Our stereotypes may reflect ourselves rather than others. Perhaps the first rule for understanding people is to accept that they may be different from ourselves. The second rule is to treat people as individuals and to be prepared for the unexpected. Use frameworks as guides not straitjackets.

Rational economic stereotype

This view sees people as mainly motivated by economic incentives so that individuals will always act in a calculating way to maximize economic gain for themselves, in preference to all other rewards at work. People are seen as passive agents to be stimulated to perform well by money incentives. Feelings are to be discounted and controlled, because they may get in the way of the monetary self-interest calculation.

These assumptions underlie many economic theories and form the basis of a large number of organizational cultures. Heavy reliance upon this stereotype will place emphasis upon doing things 'to' people to get efficiency, upon money incentives and competition and upon close supervision and control of staff. It will discount the importance of relationships, feelings and job satisfaction at work.

Social stereotype

This stereotype sees people dominated by social needs to belong, to feel part of a group, to display loyalty and to give and receive friendship, acceptance and support from others at work. An individual's dominant experience at work is relationships with individuals and groups.

These assumptions are common in organizations which place great emphasis on human relationships at work. This stresses the importance of paying attention to the needs of people, to understanding their feelings and to harnessing the individual's need to identify with the group, department or organization. It discounts the influence of material incentives and job satisfaction at work.

Self-fulfilment stereotype

This generalization indicates that people are mainly influenced by the need to develop their abilities and use their particular skills to the full. This is associated with self-motivation in a climate which allows independence and responsibility. Work should provide opportunities for self-fulfilment. Jobs should have variety and challenge.

This view is common in organizations with a high proportion of staff working to professional codes. It highlights 'intrinsic' satisfaction derived from the tasks and responsibilities which make up a job. Focus is upon delegation, training and ways of creating job satisfaction. It discounts the material side of a person's career and gives low priority to relationships and other needs that individuals may have.

Understanding without stereotypes: complex people

The trouble with stereotypes is that, although the individual holding them believes they are 'true', they only fit some people well, others only partly and many people not at all. It is best to start from the basis that people are complex, highly variable and that individuals develop and change as a result of internal processes and external factors.

It is important that we do not oversimplify when we attempt to understand a person. Even if we think we know them well, we should always be prepared for surprises.

There are a number of frameworks in later chapters which help us understand people and their complexity. One approach to the links between personality and behaviour is the work of A H Maslow. This gets to grips with the variety and dynamic nature of human motives and behaviour. His need hierarchy suggests that there are a range of needs which evolve as the individual is more or less successful in meeting them. This evolution brings out different motives and goals so that facets of the individual emerge or retreat over time. His ideas can help us understand ourselves and others.

The need hierarchy

Maslow suggests that human needs operate in the form of a hierarchy with basic needs influencing goals and behaviour until they are more or less satisfied in the individual's environment, when the next need would emerge as an important influence.

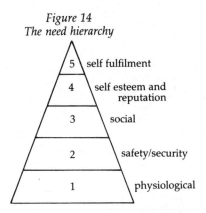

Figure 14
The need hierarchy

5 self fulfilment

4 self esteem and reputation

3 social

2 safety/security

1 physiological

1 *Physiological needs* Physiological needs such as hunger, thirst, sex and shelter are the first-level needs. If these appetites are not satisfied in the circumstances of the person's life, then they will dominate that person's thinking, feeling, goals and behaviour. If they are more or less satisfied on a regular basis, then the next level of need will emerge as a dominant factor.

2 *Safety/security needs* These relate to avoidance of danger, threat and deprivation as well as minimizing anxiety and uncertainty. If the individual feels physically and emotionally secure then the next level emerges.

3 *Social needs* As physiological and security needs are more or less satisfied, the individual begins to be increasingly aware of social needs. As with other needs, these are translated into personal goals which influence the individual's behaviour and interests. Social needs involve giving and receiving friendship, acceptance, support, loyalty, social anchorage and love. Again, once these are met to a degree in the individual's circumstances, the next level of needs makes itself known.

4 *Self-esteem and reputation needs* Self-esteem needs are concerned

Figure 15: Needs and personal goals examples

COMMON BASIC NEEDS	COMMON BASIC PERSONAL GOALS	SPECIFIC PERSONAL GOALS
SELF FULFILMENT	1 Increase in power over people/situations responsibility 2 Increase in autonomy. To be self directed 3 Increase in the use and development of valued abilities 4 An environment with sufficient variety of stimulus	If the needs are active, they will manifest themselves in a variety of ways. For some individuals it may be sufficient to have varied tasks; some may wish to develop specialized abilities and skills; others may prefer power or responsibility
SELF ESTEEM	1 Achievement of personal standards 2 Enhancement of sense of personal worth	Standards and self-concepts vary from individual to individual. They are often the internalization of the perceived opinions of other people who are 'valued' by the individual (eg 'Give a dog a bad name . . .')
REPUTATION	Enhancement of individual's standing with those whose recognition and respect he values 1 Increase in prestige, through behaviour or accomplishment approved by those people he values 2 Increase in status ('office' or symbols of office)	The people or group whose respect is valued will vary from individual to individual. The means of gaining respect will also vary. The 'reference figure' may be symbolic (eg 'If only X could see me now')
SOCIAL	Achievement of social anchorage, acceptance, friendship through contact with others and membership A focus for commitment, identification, loyalty	Individual variation in desired anchorage points, desired sources of friendship. They may be colleagues, superiors, 'outside' groups, family or a mix of them all. The focus of an individual's commitment etc will also vary between individuals
SECURITY/SAFETY	1 Avoidance of physical deprivation 2 Avoidance of threats of deprivation which the individual feels he has no chance of controlling 3 Avoidance of stress which produces anxiety 4 Knowing where you stand	Perception of danger varies Perception of what is controllable by 'self' varies Anxiety 'threshold' and the causes of anxiety varies
PHYSIOLOGICAL	1 Hunger 2 Thirst 3 Sex 4 Shelter	Basic requirements (eg survival) may be common to all. As with all other needs, the degree of need (appetites), and the means of achieving goals (taste) vary. It is obvious that not all needs will be met within the work environment.

INDIVIDUAL TRANSLATION OF NEEDS INTO PERSONAL GOALS:
Basic 'needs' may be common to all men, but they are translated into 'goal profiles' which will be unique to each individual; goals have a direct influence on behaviour, being the 'object' of behaviour/action

with enhancement of self-image, meeting personal standards, self-respect and achievement. The individual will also become increasingly interested in reputation, status and their standing with those whose recognition and respect are valued.

5 *Self-fulfilment needs* These relate to fully achieving personal potential, using talents that the individual enjoys and for continuous growth and development. It is likely that these are rarely satisfied.

Not only will people's need profiles vary, but so will tastes and appetites. Taste refers to preferred ways of meeting a need and appetite refers to the amount a person has of a particular need. It is also likely that the need sequence will vary for some people, although the range of needs may be common. Needs are translated into 'goal profiles' unique to each individual, some examples of which are illustrated in figure 15 on page 48.

Activity plan 4
Using the following needs/goals profile form, either:

(a) Make an assessment of your own 'personal goals' profile. How does this relate to your behaviour?
(b) Get a colleague or friend to work with you. Each will ask his partner questions about himself and his job, so that each of you can gather information in order to make an assessment of the other's needs and 'personal goal' profiles. On the basis of this each partner in turn should describe the work situation that he feels is at present appropriate for the other; each should comment on the way the other behaves and reacts in his present job.
(c) Make an assessment of at least one of your subordinate's 'personal goals' profiles. How does this explain the way she presently behaves and reacts?

Needs/goals profile form

BASIC NEEDS* Scale score range		PERSONAL GOALS List those you think you have identified
1 inactive	6 highly active	
	score 1–6	
SELF FULFILMENT		
SELF ESTEEM		
REPUTATION		
SOCIAL		
SECURITY/SAFETY		
PHYSICAL		

* There are three kinds of 'need states' for any category
ACTIVE Emerged, but not fully satisfied; therefore a focus of the individual's current behaviour, aspirations and goals. High score
DORMANT/SATISFIED Emerged, but is currently well satisfied in the individual's current life circumstances; because of this it is not a significant focus of the individual's current behaviour, aspirations and goals. Low/moderate score. (NB If the individual's circumstances change, this need could re-emerge as 'active')
DORMANT/LATENT Has not yet emerged as a strong force within the individual, and is therefore not a significant focus of the individual's current behaviour, aspirations and goals. Low score. (NB If the individual's circumstances change, so that other active needs become 'fully' satisfied, this need may begin to emerge as 'active')

50

4 Managing learning, development and performance

It is part of the manager's job to help people develop, both for their current roles and future careers. This chapter examines how people learn to tackle new responsibilities and develop skills to enhance performance. It also looks at things managers and organizations can do to assist this process.

Investing in people: learning not teaching

We live in turbulent times. Changes occur frequently in our organizations, our jobs and the way we perform them. It is more important than ever that the manager helps people to grow in confidence, develop new skills and cope with the challenges of change.

People are the most important resource and investment in them will produce great benefit. This involves investing money and time in staff development not just as an organizational system run by a personnel or training department, but more importantly as a central part of every manager's job. Most people recognized as 'effective managers' not only have departments with consistently good results, but also will be seen to be helping their staff develop and perform well. However, research conducted by Robin Evenden during the last decade continues to show that the substantial majority of managers have a technical rather than people focus to their role, and this is reflected in a low priority given to people development.

There are many reasons for the manager's low level of involvement in developing the 'human resource'. It is partly that they do not define their roles in these terms, although the Training Commission's emphasis on the manager's integral training role suggests that there are significant attempts being made to change this.

51

Another reason for managers avoiding responsibility in this area is their lack of confidence in their capacity to influence staff development. This is frequently the result of a very narrow view of how people can be helped to develop. Often development is seen to be the same as training, training seen to be the same as teaching and the manager feels inadequate as a teacher. Development is much more than training, training is more than teaching and managers can do a great deal to help staff develop without needing to become teachers. The secret is to see development as helping people to learn, and there are many ways to do this.

The first step is to consider how people learn. Do we all learn in the same way? If there are differences in the way we learn, what are they? Can people inhibit their own learning? Do managers and organizations inhibit learning?

How do people learn?

Activity plan 1: how did you learn?
A useful start to understanding learning is to consider the way we ourselves learn. It is suggested that you think about your own learning during your life, perhaps during your own work career. Think about things that happened, projects that you undertook, incidents, other people who were involved with you and your own approach and feelings about what was going on.

1 Identify a period when your role changed, perhaps upon starting a new job or being promoted, *and you learned a great deal.*
   1.1 Note what you learned and how you learned it. Think broadly about your learning. Include skills, knowledge and also 'know-how'; 'fitting-in', getting to know the new rules and group norms; finding our what was expected from you; 'learning the ropes' and so on. How did you do it?
   1.2 Identify one other person who was particularly significant during this period. Can you identify five or six things that person did which helped you to learn?
2 Identify another period *when you learned very little.*
   2.1 Ask yourself why you didn't learn. What was different from 1.1 above?
   2.2 Identify one person who was significant during this low learning period. Can you identify five or six things that person did or did not do which hindered your learning?

It would be interesting if you are able to compare your findings with others, noting similarities and differences.

Does it tell you anything about the way you learn (or don't learn)?

Does it suggest approaches which can help others learn?
What should be avoided so that others' learning is not hindered?

These aspects will be explored during the remainder of this chapter.

Activity plan 2: learning styles

David Kolb has made a scientific study of the way different people learn and he has produced an interesting model of learning styles which describes these differences.

You might wish to think about your own learning style, compare it with others, and think about the implications for helping yourself and others learn in the future. The following questionnaire, unlike that developed by Kolb, is not intended to be a scientific instrument, but like others in this book it is a device to help you reflect upon your own approach. When answering, you will find it helpful to think about situations when you are aware that you have learned things.

Instructions

There are six sets of four words listed below. Working across the page rank each word 1–4. The word ranked 4 will be the one which best describes the way you learn. The word ranked 1 will least characterize it.

1 – involved	– observes	– logical	– testing
2 – enthusiastic	– thoughtful	– analytical	– practical
3 – intuitive	– reflective	– systematic	– tries out
4 – feelings	– listening	– clarity	– new ideas
5 – receptive	– stands back	– rational	– seeks evidence
6 – challenging	– gathers data	– explanation	– takes risks
Total A ——	B ——	C ——	D ——

Add the four columns, so that you have a score for A, B, C and D.

A EXPERIENCE — This suggests involvement in the things going on around you and the enjoyment of experience. It indicates being concerned with the present, being open-minded and emotionally expressive. Learning by being part of what is happening.

B REFLECTION — This implies thinking about your experience. Standing back, taking time out to reflect, not rushing into conclusions. Ruminating. Learning by reflecting about what has happened.

C CONCEPTS — This involves drawing conclusions from

53

having reflected upon your experience. It is the analysis of what has happened and gathering together of ideas, concepts, theories, frameworks or guidelines for action.

D EXPERIMENTING This means testing out the rules and principles in action. Seeing if they work. Looking for new ideas and solutions. Taking nothing for granted. Seeing what happens if you do it differently. Learning by trial and error.

Figure 16
Your learning style preference profile

The four lines below are marked A, B, C, D and correspond to your questionnaire scores. By marking in your scores and connecting the points you will have a representation of your learning style preferences.

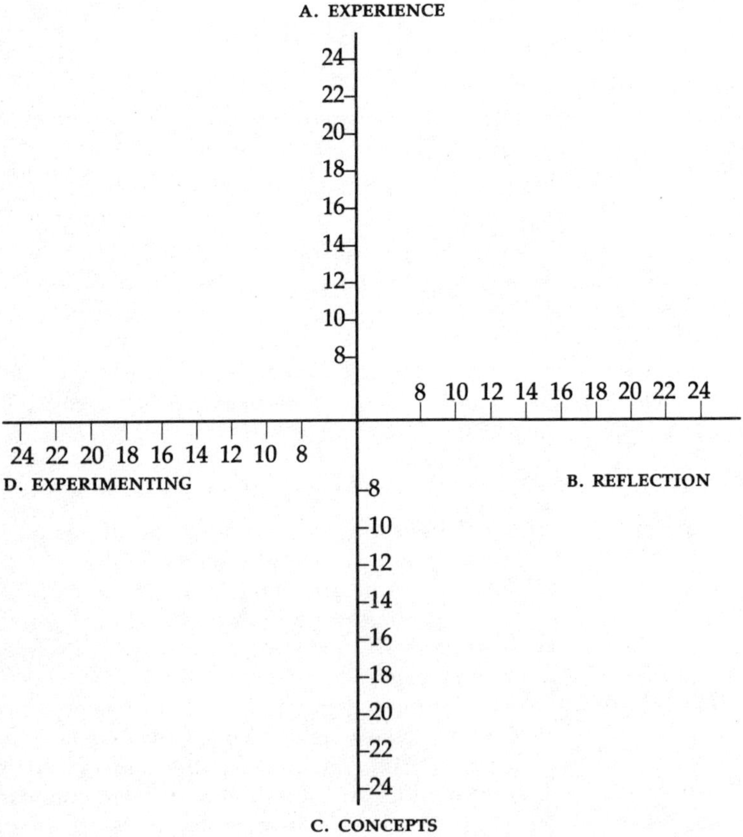

A. EXPERIENCE

```
24
22
20
18
16
14
12
10
 8
                    8  10 12 14 16 18 20 22 24
```

```
24 22 20 18 16 14 12 10  8
D. EXPERIMENTING                          B. REFLECTION
                         8
                        10
                        12
                        14
                        16
                        18
                        20
                        22
                        24
```

C. CONCEPTS

The four points on the profile represent the learning process, or cycle, which is based upon that described by David Kolb. Your high scores give clues about the learning modes you prefer whilst the lower scores may reflect those least preferred.

All four modes are important for learning and if you have marked differences between them you might want to consider what new learning opportunities you might achieve by altering your profile or helping others develop theirs. When learning, we move around the cycle in a continuous process. If we skip a stage, or give it a low priority, our learning will be restricted and problems might result from it. For example, an individual who is very strong at reflecting and conceptualizing may be weak at putting ideas into practice, testing things out or accepting new ways of doing things. Alternatively, a person who actively tries out new things and lives in the present may make costly mistakes and, perhaps even worse, will not learn from them.

1 THE BROADCASTER
(The Experience/Reflection quadrant)

Reflects on experience and enjoys it. Produces a multitude of widely scattered points and problems, often not related to each other. Usually aware of what is happening in the present. A good witness/observer.

A 'butterfly' mind. Has difficulty prioritizing decisions/actions in terms of importance and urgency. Does not examine anything closely, plan or try things out.

2 THE PUZZLER
(The Reflection/Concepts quadrant)

Reflects at length on ideas and problems. Enjoys abstract analysis and defining. Likes to puzzle and search for the right answer.

Can suffer from 'analysis-paralysis'. Does not get beyond ideas to planning and action. May have a limited view of situations and get stuck with looking for the perfect answer. Thinks about new approaches but may not try them out.

3 THE JUDGE
(The Concepts/Experimenting quadrant)

Assesses ideas and selects solutions. Enjoys drawing conclusions and making judgements. Tests concepts intellectually. Establishes priorities.

Tends to make snap judgements without considering enough options. May define problems too narrowly and not use the experience of others. Could be more concerned with assessing ideas than creating them.

4 THE EXECUTOR
(The Experimenting/Experience quadrant)

Puts a great deal of energy into doing things. Tries out new ideas. Likes to get things completed. Enjoys activity. Lives in the present and expresses feelings.

Often acts without thinking. Mistakes can result from lack of planning. May repeat mistakes. Can operate unpredictably and spread confusion.

If you are helping others to learn, it is important to accept that they may learn differently from you. You may need to explore many ways to facilitate learning. A development programme should include a variety of approaches to suit each individual. A range of methods which can help people learn will be examined shortly as will ways of helping to identify and overcome blocks to learning which can stunt development.

Activity plan 3: positive support for learning
Perhaps using ideas from the previous Action Plans, identify some ways that the four different learning style preferences could be met. Think about things you could do to help others learn. Compare notes with colleagues if you have the opportunity. Remember, you can facilitate learning by:

      1 meeting an individual's learning preferences

and 2 helping an individual learn in new ways, by encouraging them to understand their profile and try out least preferred modes

Methods of staff development

Courses
A well-run and appropriate training course will be an effective part of an individual's learning and development, but it is unlikely to succeed in isolation from other supporting conditions.

1 Has the need for development been accurately identified?
2 Has it been discussed and agreed with the individual?
3 Can you help the individual develop a positive attitude to the course?
4 Will you discuss the course and what can be gained from it prior to the attendance?
5 Are you both sure it is the right course?
6 Are individuals encouraged to transfer learning through an action plan?

56

Figure 17
Examples of positive support for different learning preferences

LEARNING STYLE PREFERENCES	EXAMPLES
A EXPERIENCE	1 Give opportunities for a range of experiences. 2 Offer a variety of tasks. 3 Discuss the individual's experience of work, problems, achievement and feelings. 4 Encourage involvement in job-related events. 5 Share experience.
B REFLECTION	1 Encourage the person to stand back and think about job-related experience. 2 Ask open-ended questions which prompt reflection. 3 Set reflective and descriptive tasks, such as reading and commenting on reports. 4 Encourage recording, diaries, progress reports. 5 Exchange reflections.
C CONCEPTS	1 Offer frameworks, principles, guidelines. 2 Seek explanations from the person. 3 Encourage the individual to see relationships. 4 Ask the person to 'teach' you or others. 5 Exchange ideas.
D EXPERIMENTING	1 Encourage new actions. 2 Support activity testing by giving recognition. 3 Don't blame, but help people learn from mistakes. 4 Ask the individual what they are doing differently. 5 Share experiments.

7 Will you discuss the action plan and provide support after the course?
8 Will the individual have opportunity to put into practice new ideas, knowledge and skills?
9 Do you need to develop to help your staff develop?

The outcome of even the best courses will be minimized if these conditions are not met.

Example
People learn a great deal from the example of others and this can be used to good effect. You may be an effective role model yourself or you may be able to identify others who are. Judicious use of exemplars can be a powerful learning tool. One problem is that the person learning may pick up the bad practices along with the good, so monitoring and additional guidance may be necessary.

Coaching and mentoring
Coaching and mentoring are very similar methods. They both involve one person helping another to develop into a job or career. The differences are that coaching is often seen as the role of an individual's manager, whereas mentoring is a system whereby the individual is taken under the wing of an experienced person who is not the boss and is probably in another part of the organization or outside it.

Mentoring involves giving advice, counselling, support and generally helping the protégé get on. It can be very effective, especially if the relationship is based upon trust and confidentiality. Its advantage is that the mentor has no line authority over the individual and so the relationship can be detached from the personal needs and interests of the boss. For example, the mentor may encourage the individual to seek career development outside the department, something which many line managers are reluctant to do.

Coaching is something all managers should undertake either to remedy an individual's performance problem or to develop new skills and approaches. In terms of the 'learning cycle', it involves a manager working with subordinates to ensure they become aware of problems or development needs, reflect upon them and develop a coherent picture in order to identify approaches to try out in practice. This is performance coaching. An individual's learning and problem-solving styles can be matched or challenged in the coaching situation. Matching is useful to build on the individual's strengths, but challenging is usually needed at some point to eliminate the weaknesses in a particular learning style.

58

Figure 18
Performance coaching styles: matching and challenging

EXPERIENCE

Coaching the EXECUTOR
Supporting coaching style:

THE ACTIVATOR
Energizes. Comes straight to the point. Recommends things to do. Offers solutions from experience. Joins in the action and may demonstrate the right way. Encourages implementation.

Challenging coaching styles:
1 Reviewer   2 ANALYST
3 Planning prioritizer

EXPERIMENTING

Coaching the BROADCASTER
Supporting coaching style:

THE REVIEWER
Shares experiences and asks open-ended questions in a non-directive way. Encourages an exploration and review of feelings and experience.

Challenging coaching styles:
1 Analyst   2 PLANNING PRIORITIZER   3 Activator

REFLECTION

Coaching the JUDGE
Supporting coaching style:

THE PLANNING PRIORITIZER
Offers solutions and makes judgements. Seeks and offers suggestions for future action. Identifies what is urgent and important. Encourages action planning. Focuser.

Challenging coaching styles:
1 Activator   2 REVIEWER
3 Analyst

Coaching the PUZZLER
Supporting coaching style:

THE ANALYST
Offers and challenges ideas. Logical. Asks probing questions. Reduces ambiguity and seeks clarity. Looks for patterns. Offers principles and guidelines. Stimulates systematic thought.

Challenging coaching styles:
1 Planning prioritizer
2 ACTIVATOR
3 Reviewer

CONCEPTS

© Robin Evenden 1988

Coaching can begin from the learner's strong position or learning style preference and over time move round the cycle. The greatest difficulties and learning potential are likely to be at the position diagonally opposite to the individual's preferred style (*see* figure 18).

Coaching should not be treated as if it was something divorced from normal events, but should be part of the day to day contact between boss and subordinate. The process will benefit from good relations, mutual respect, planning, good assessment, action planning and feedback. It is best seen as a shared process with both parties willing to learn from each other.

Assessment and action planning

In order for people to develop, they need to identify where they are starting from, where they need to get to, how they are going to get there and how well they are doing on the way. This involves

performance assessment
feedback
action planning
monitoring the plan

Assessment It is important to gain a complete picture of each person's performance level. Some useful sources of information and evidence are previous records, comparison with others in similar jobs, impact on other people, other people's views, achievement of tasks and deadlines, sampling work—quality, quantity, speed, accuracy—and the individual's own views about their performance.

It is important to have evidence and to be clear in your own mind before communicating it to others. Five methods are

1 Simple labelling	eg good/bad, acceptable/unacceptable.
2 Descriptive	eg always/frequently/occasionally/never
3 Numerical	eg excellent poor

$$\begin{array}{ccccc} | & | & | & | & | \\ 1 & 2 & 3 & 4 & 5 \end{array}$$

4 Grading

eg A—exceeds requirements in all respects
  B—meets all requirements
  C—meets some requirements
  D—fails to meet requirements

5 Reporting—either written or verbal, describing the individual and performance, structuring it around areas of concern as well as positive aspects.

60

Feedback Bring the assessment to the attention of the individual. Focus upon what the person is doing and how they are performing, trying to avoid 'personal' remarks. Try to give observations and evidence. Be prepared to check your assumptions and make sure the feedback has been clearly received.

Figure 19
Feedback skills: coaching and assessment

1 *Focus on behaviour rather than the person.* The receiver will feel less threatened and that you are discussing things that can be changed.

2 *Describe rather than judge.* A description in neutral terms may lead to acceptance. A judgement, on the other hand, in terms of good or bad, right or wrong, may produce defensive rejection. Focus what the other person does, not what you feel about it.

3 *Give feedback close to the event.* It is likely to have more impact and meaning if it is given in concrete terms when the experience is still fresh.

4 *Look at behaviour which the person can do something about.* It is pointless and frustrating to focus on things that the person can do nothing about.

5 *Check that the feedback has been clear.* Ask the receiver to summarize the feedback to see if it corresponds with the giver's intentions.

Action planning After discussing the performance feedback it is important to agree an action plan which clearly identifies what is to be done and how it is to be achieved. It helps to prioritize by identifying the most important things to be done and the most urgent. Selecting support requirements, including your own rôle, should also be part of action planning: for example, training, coaching, resources, encouragement, recognition and job change. Try to specify in concrete terms what is to be achieved and include target times. Set a series of achievable objectives which lead steadily to the desired level of improvement.

Monitoring the plan Ask the individual to self-monitor the plan and, if appropriate, seek guidance from you as necessary. It is important that the individual has responsibility for the plan and its achievement, but it is necessary to check progress, not least to provide encouragement and demonstrate interest. Continue to sample and assess the individual's performance.

Planned experience

Development can be inhibited by the boundaries of a particular job. This can be overcome by agreeing with individuals' planned developmental experiences.

Projects Special assignments, for example investigating specific problems and identifying solutions, could add to an individual's skill and experience.

Temporary upgrading This involves individuals taking over the responsibilities of others, perhaps more senior, at times of holidays and illness. It is important to treat this as a learning experience, and not just emergency cover. It is also important to share the temporary upgradings amongst those who would benefit and to make sure that it is not interpreted as a promise of promotion.

Job rotation Variety of tasks can be motivating and is discussed in the Motivation chapter as 'job enrichment'. However, it can also have clear developmental advantages.

Secondment This is being used increasingly as a means of developing management potential as part of an organization's development plan. It could mean planned moves to other functions or departments or even to other organizations. The aim is to prepare the individual for different and broader responsibilities in the future.

Delegation

Delegation is a core management tool which not only affects an individual's development but is also central to motivation, time management and performance effectiveness. It is one of the most important things that a manager should do and it is frequently handled inadequately.

Delegation does not mean 'passing the buck'. You do not delegate accountability, but authority to act and decide within defined limits. The scope you give to a subordinate will need to be related to your use of other management skills such as assessment, coaching and support.

The experience of exercising authority and responsibility under the supportive guidance of a manager, who does not 'over-supervise', is probably the most powerful single means of development.

Activity plan 4: are you good at delegation?

This is a self-assessment exercise. It is not a scientific instrument but is designed to help you think about how you delegate.

Don't spend too much time reflecting on a question.

Place one tick at the appropriate point on the scale. 'Yes' is '0', 'Often' is '1', 'Sometimes' is '2' and 'No' is '3'.

		Yes 0	1	2	No 3
1	Do you work at home?				
2	Do you spend too much time on work you did prior to promotion?				
3	Do you miss deadlines?				
4	Are you the last person to leave the office?				
5	Do you sign all your section/group's mail/memos?				
6	Are you frequently interrupted by questions from your subordinates?				
7	Would you say half your work is routine?				
8	Is your desk full when you return after absence?				
9	Is it difficult to find time for your subordinates?				
10	Do you find it hard to accept less than high standards from subordinates?				
11	Are you involved in everything that happens in your section/group?				
12	Do you get annoyed if subordinates do not immediately understand you?				
13	Are you a little jealous if a subordinate gets praise from somebody else?				
14	Do you interrupt subordinates with work to be done immediately?				
15	Do you alter subordinates' decisions/solutions in aspects you have delegated?				
	TOTALS				

Marking
1 Write in the marks for each tick, eg a 'no' tick equals 3.
2 Add the marks in each column.
3 Add the column totals together.

Figure 20
Causes of poor delegation and some solutions

1	Lack of confidence in subordinates.	Build up your confidence by developing and encouraging them.
2	Over-supervision.	Aim to focus on their results rather than the details of what they do.
3	Delegated authority does not match responsibility.	Discuss this with subordinates. Make sure authority and responsibility limits are clear.
4	Subordinates lack confidence.	Give them support and encouragement.
5	Fear that subordinates will do a better job than you.	Accept that subordinate's performance reflects well on you.
6	You feel you can do it better.	It is not what you are paid for. Help them to improve.
7	You like doing the subordinate's job.	Master management skills rather than job skills. You may enjoy that too.
8	Subordinates are under great pressure.	Help them prioritize and become more efficient. Make realistic demands.
9	Unclear instructions, authority, deadlines, etc	Have a 'delegation' checklist for each 'project'. Make sure you both understand and agree it.
10	Subordinates are left in the dark or isolated.	Remember that delegation is not abdication. Monitor results and progress.

Scores

0– 5 You are probably kidding yourself.

6–20 Not too good. Worth brushing up on your delegation technique.

21–30 OK, but some areas to work on.
31–40 You delegate well.
41–45 You are probably kidding yourself.

How to delegate

1 Establish your own key jobs and those of your subordinates.
2 Identify the decisions/solutions/task areas which will be a subordinate's responsibility.
3 Give necessary instructions.
4 Check that subordinates have the authority to make decisions, and know that they have it.
5 Decide what monitoring you need.
6 Decide upon deadlines.
7 Agree the above with your subordinates. Check mutual understanding.
8 Get to know your subordinate's personal and technical skills.
9 Develop your subordinates by
   letting them know what you expect
   listening to them
   assessing them and giving constructive feedback
   building their confidence
   giving them recognition
   giving them the benefit of your experience but not doing it for them
10 Do not accept 'problems' from your subordinates, only 'solutions'.
11 Don't allow subordinates to delegate upwards.
12 The above will minimize mistakes, but they will happen. Help your subordinates to learn from them.
13 Encourage your boss to delegate in the same way. Your boss will want the same from you, that you want from your subordinates.

Formal qualifications and professional associations

Many organizations encourage study for technical and professional qualifications and in recent years the traditional approach has been supplemented by distance and open learning. Self-study opportunities have increased enormously and major examples are the Open University and Open Tech. A good example is the distance-learning MBA offered by the University of Strathclyde Business School. Audio-visual aids, computers, databases, electronic mail and television have led to an explosion of self-study packages.

Most professional associations emphasize continuous development and provide ways of doing this, either through advice or training. The activities of many professional bodies often include

Figure 21
Overcoming blocks to learning and development

PERSONAL BLOCKS	BLOCK-REDUCING/REMOVING: EXAMPLES OF ACTION
CLOSED MIND Unable to see things or recognize what is happening in potential learning situations.	Ask how the individual sees things? Suggest alternatives. Point out how to look for learning opportunities.
NORMATIVE Internalized 'norms' about what is 'done' or 'not done' which may cause avoidance of learning opportunities.	Find out what learning-related norms the individual may have and discuss them, eg 'Graduates are above that sort of thing', 'Keep your ideas/opinions to yourself', 'Stick to the rules and don't take chances'.
EMOTIONAL Anxiety; avoidance; over-dependence; discounts feedback on emotive, non-rational grounds; lacks confidence.	Provide support; help relax. Encourage the acceptance of feedback. Give feedback, eg 'I see you avoiding things'. Promote self-reliance and confidence. Counsel; get close to. Check your own approach to the individual.
RELATIONAL Aggressive; shy; abrasive; rebellious; difficult; non-collaborative; relationship problems limit the chance to learn from others.	Give feedback—'I see you as . . .' *and* seek feedback, 'We don't get on too well'. (Relationships are two-sided.) Check your own approach. Counsel and guide.
MOTIVATIONAL Personal goals frustrated; switched off; resistance to learning; low enthusiasm; demoralization.	Find out what the individual wants to learn. Jointly set performance criteria and targets. Encourage and support. Set real and realistic projects. Provide opportunity for motivational rewards. Avoid 'switch-off' factors.
LEARNING Learning behaviours associated with a particular learning style are inappropriate.	Encourage reflection on how the individual learns; suggest additional ways. Stimulate; challenge; give feedback.

meetings, exhibitions and conferences which provide not only opportunities to increase knowledge but also development through shared experience.

Self-managed learning

One of the more recent approaches to development is the encouragement of individuals to take responsibility for it themselves. Traditional providers of training and development, such as colleges and training departments, become resources to be used and managed by individuals in a non-dependent fashion. This requires some adjustment from all parties used to more traditional modes of learning, but early evidence suggests that this can be a very powerful form of development, which may have long-term benefits to the individual, particularly in terms of initiating and growing into change.

Overcoming blocks to learning and development

An individual's learning can be restricted by blocks from within the individual or from external factors. Another person may help the individual remove or reduce these blocks.

Figure 22
Organizational blocks to learning for an individual: structural blocks

EXPERIENCE
activities routine,
ritualistic, predictable,
uninvolving; unclear
standards.

EXPERIMENTING
Prescribed duties,
methods; rules,
procedures, 'red tape',
high cost of failure.

REFLECTION
Poor communications,
inadequate feedback,
isolation, fast pace.

CONCEPTS
Emphasis on results, short
time-scale, disjointed,
interruptions, lack of 'post-
mortems' & think-tank
procedures.

Figure 23
Organizational blocks to learning for an individual: cultural blocks

---

EXPERIENCE
Preference for
distance detachment.
Us/them—don't get
hands dirty.
Ivory tower.

EXPERIMENTING
Tread carefully.
Don't rock the boat—
it's highly political.

REFLECTION
Present-orientated.
Don't live in the past.
Let's get on with today.

CONCEPTS
Thinking is for academics.
It's results that count.
No use sitting around
on your backside.

Development can occur as a result of recognizing organizational blocks to learning and taking positive action to overcome them. It is likely that successful organizations of the future will be those which are able to become 'learning communities' as well as 'working communities'.

5 Interpersonal relations: getting on with others

It has become a truism that a manager achieves results through other people. The quality of relationships in terms of influencing and interacting with others is crucial. In the first part of this chapter ways of understanding how these relationships can be made productive or otherwise are explored. As usual the text is followed by an activity plan so that the understanding can be tested out and used in real life.

A manager's effectiveness depends on much more than technical experience and knowledge. Being a T-type manager is not enough. Managers rarely work in isolation; a large part of their job is involved with relationships with their subordinates, their boss and their colleagues, both on a one-to-one basis and within a group. Thus effectiveness will depend largely on the quality of interpersonal relationships.

We all know people who manage to achieve highly by evoking the active cooperation of others; equally we can all identify managers who, despite their general competence, don't achieve to the level their abilities would suggest. It is as though the resources they have are prevented from being used effectively because somehow something happens in the quality of the interactions and communications that occur between themselves and others. It is this something, particularly awareness of self and others, on which your success and failure in achieving things with and through other people will depend. The crucial factor is the perception you have of yourself and other people—that is, the extent to which you see yourself as others see you. Equally important is how far you see others as they see themselves.

This is a complex business because we react to not only what is said but use our perceptions to interpret the subtle clues to get the real message. Sometimes double messages are sent which may seem to be contradictory. For instance, a person may argue against a proposal because he feels he must defend a group he represents, but he argues in such a way as to let it be known that he privately prefers to be convinced and will go along eventually. Often we say one thing in order to save face but manage to communicate something else.

Double messages of which the sender is aware do not usually pose difficulties. Greater difficulty arises from double messages, whether from ourselves or others, of which we are unaware. In looking at the perceptions we have of ourselves and others it is useful to think of a person as having several parts (figure 24).

Figure 24
The parts of a person: the Johari window

Open self	Blind self
Concealed self	Unknown self

The perception of self consists of two components.

Open self
The 'you' you are aware of and are willing to share or reveal.

Concealed self
Knowledge of yourself which you choose to conceal from others, such as feelings of insecurity, reactions to others or antisocial feelings. Usually concealed are factors which are inconsistent with the self-image you have of yourself.

Blind self
The open and concealed self combined is how a person sees himself—his self perception—but it is not the full story. Other people's perceptions of us will not correspond exactly with the image we try to project. In addition they perceive some of our blind self—an impression of us with which we may be unacquainted.

The blind self are those things which we unconsciously conceal from ourselves which yet are part of us and which are communicated to others. For instance, each of us has feelings and traits which we feel are not part of us. We may be blind to the fact that some of these feelings leak out and are communicated to others.

Unknown self

Additionally, there is the unknown self—a part of us of which nobody is aware, such as truly unconscious and deeply repressed feelings and impulses, hidden talents, potentialities, skills etc.

There is much valuable loss of communication when there is conscious concealment of reactions to interpersonal events. For example, one of your co-workers may feel that a presentation you made went badly wrong, but withholds her reactions in order not to hurt your feelings or make you angry. Equally, one of your subordinates may irritate you by what you regard as patronizing behaviour but, instead of 'levelling' with him, out of politeness, you choose to endure this behaviour and mask your feelings, irrespective of the fact that he is likely to alienate others. Should feedback be given, however, this has the effect of reducing the blind and increasing the open self.

Figure 25
Effect of feedback and disclosure on the Johari Window

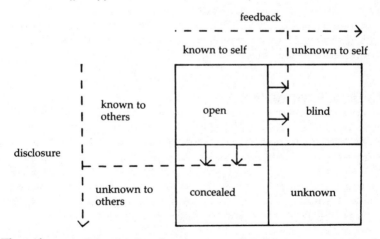

Thus if communication can be encouraged to be open and honest, not concealing feelings out of politeness or because it is the thing to do, this provides the context in which interpersonal relations can become effective.

71

Disclosure, where the open self replaces some of the concealed self (figure 25 above), also affects the quality of interpersonal relations. Within an organizational setting disclosure is important and helpful as long as it is relevant to the operation of the organization. Again, as people disclose the way they think and feel and are more open about these things, this heightens the quality of communication.

We can add, too, to our own feedback by developing a sensitivity to the clues about the way others perceive us and our influence on them. The more we get to know about ourselves the more effective are we likely to become. One of the activities at the end of the chapter will help in that it will enable you to get a fix on the way some others perceive you.

We are not advocating of course that the manager changes style in an abrupt and dramatic fashion from concealment to openness, feedback and disclosure, as it is likely that this would produce an equally dramatic result but of the wrong kind. Sometimes such a transformation can be made when the whole group undergoes a training experience concerned with developing openness, but what happens here is that the group come to share a common climate about its value. Even so if feedback is gratuitously given to a member of some other group that doesn't share these values, some risk is incurred.

The values held about it are thus essential to successful feedback and openness; the manager can develop this openness as a gradual process so that people come to share a climate that encourages it. On a personal level the more we know about ourselves and the reactions of others—that is, the more open we are to the environment of other people with whom we interact, the more successful we are likely to be.

Transactional analysis

A further approach to enhancing understanding of relationships and interactions between people is that of transactional analysis (TA). TA has received wide currency in recent years, not only as a way of giving insights into the way people interact but also as a theory of personality and as a tool for therapy. It is not the intent here to consider it for these two latter purposes, but only as a background to gaining greater understanding and skill in interacting with others. For many the approach provides vivid additional insight.

One difficulty is with the language. The originators of TA set out to describe in everyday language what is after all a complex theory of personality. While the aim is to be applauded, some find the terminology used confusing because a word may have a different meaning from that of everyday usage; others find the jargon irritating and distracting. Because the reader may want to read more widely in this area the conventional language used in TA has been retained here.

In essence TA is concerned with recognizing and understanding the basic modes of behaviour individuals take up and from which their interactions (or transactions) emanate, the various kinds of transactions and how to deal with them. It is also concerned with the underlying reasons for the behaviour and psychological games with an ulterior pay-off into which people frequently try to ensnare others.

The first stage in the theory concerns ego states.

Ego states

Every individual has three basic ego states which are separate and distinct sources of behaviour: the 'parent' ego state, the 'adult' ego state and the 'child' ego state. An ego state is defined as 'a consistent pattern of feeling and experience directly related to a corresponding consistent pattern of behaviour'.

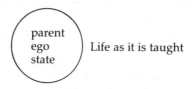

parent ego state   Life as it is taught

The 'parent' ego state contains the predisposed attitudes and opinions which are learned at a very early age, primarily from parents and other authority figures. Outwardly, it is often expressed towards others in prejudicial, critical or nurturing behaviour. Inwardly, it is experienced as old parental influences that still have an effect. These influences or data are permanently recorded in our brains and are available for replay, such as when we respond to the here and now by calling on this data.

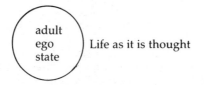

adult ego state   Life as it is thought

The 'adult' ego state is not related to a person's age. It is concerned

73

with objectively appraising reality and uses information from all sources to estimate probabilities and make statements. In many ways it is similar to a computer.

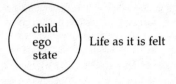

child ego state   Life as it is felt

The 'child' ego state consists of all the urges and feelings that come naturally to an individual, the recordings of his early experiences, how he responded to them and the feelings this caused, and the positions he took about himself and the others.

Thus when people are acting, feeling and thinking as they observed their parents to have done, they are in their 'parent' ego state. Their 'parent' decides for them, without reasoning how to respond to the here and now problem and other people. When they are appraising reality, gathering facts and making objective judgements, they are in their 'adult' ego state, and when feelings predominate and they feel and act as they did when children they are in their 'child' ego state.

There are no absolute rights or wrongs about behaviour from any one of the ego states. What is appropriate depends upon the nature of the interaction. Importantly too, the boundaries between the states are not rigid; rather, people tend to move from one ego state to another again depending on the situation. For this reason it is usual to show the ego states in the following diagrammatic form:

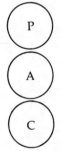

People in their parent ego state may be protective, sympathetic and nurturing on some occasions and critical, prejudicial, moralizing and punitive on others. We have two types of 'parent' in us: a 'nurturing parent' and a 'critical parent'. When we respond warmly to someone who needs help or understanding, are protective,

74

affectionate, sympathetic, loving or empathetic we are in our 'nurturing parent' state.

It is when we are in our 'critical parent' state that we are oppressive, over-controlling and prejudiced, putting others down and minimizing their problems, being dominant and controlling the situation we are in. Here we have learned to be critical of others and expect that they should measure up to our standards and views.

A boss, wife, teacher or friend who frequently uses the critical side of his 'parent state' may appear as a bossy know it all, whose behaviour intimidates, irritates or alienates other people. On the other hand, the 'critical parent' also has an important protective function, eg 'Don't cross the road without looking left and right'.

The 'child' ego state too has a number of parts. When in our *natural* child' state we express ourselves spontaneously without concern for the reactions of others, and it is the ego state we are

When in our 'natural child' state we express ourselves spontaneously without concern for the reactions of others.

in when we are having fun or being affectionate and impulsive. It reflects authentic and spontaneous feelings, including those we may not like, such as fear, anger and selfishness. We all learned, to varying degrees, to modify our natural behaviour at an early age in order to obtain what we wanted. In mature people the *'adapted* child' is expressed when we use patterns of behaviour which enable us to get along with, manipulate or get some attention from the people that matter to us. Our natural reactions are replaced by others, such as compliance, withdrawal or procrastination. The third part, the *'little professor'*, is that part which is intuitive and creative and which provides flashes of inspiration.

There are a number of clues—words, tone of voice, gestures or expressions, attitudes—to indicate which ego state a person is acting from at a particular time. For example, typical 'parent' words contain value judgements and slogans for living. Phrases that begin with 'you' usually come from the 'parent'. Some clues to indicate which ego state a person is operating from are listed in the chart on page 77.

Some people use one ego state more than the others. An 'egograph' of a person showing the percentage of his time spent in particular ego states whilst at work may be as follows:

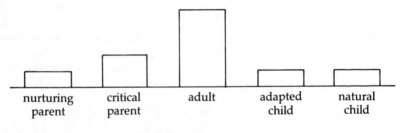

| nurturing parent | critical parent | adult | adapted child | natural child |

While at home it may be more like:

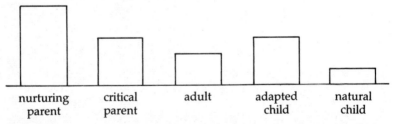

| nurturing parent | critical parent | adult | adapted child | natural child |

It is not untypical in organizations for some people to act almost exclusively from a favourite ego state so that there is an over-reliance on it. A consequence of this is they act as though in a 'constant' ego state, as they are unable to adapt to the varying situations they encounter. Their interpersonal relationships are adversely affected.

A person who operates primarily from the 'parent ego state' often treats others, even business associates, as if they were children. Such behaviour can be found in a secretary who 'takes care of' everyone's problems at the office or in a manager who

	critical parent	nurturing parent	adult	natural child	adapted child
TYPICAL WORDS USED	bad should ought must always ridiculous	good nice I love you beautiful splendid tender	correct how what why practical quantity	wow fun want won't ouch hi	can't wish try hope please thank you
TONE	critical condescending disgusted	loving comforting concerned	even	free loud energetic	whining defiant placating
NON-VERBAL CHARACTERISTICS	pointing finger frowns anger	open arms smiling accepting	thoughtful alert open	uninhibited loose spontaneous	pouting sad innocent
UNDERLYING ATTITUDES	judgemental moralistic authoritarian	understanding caring giving	erect evaluation of facts	curious fun loving changeable	demanding compliant ashamed

tries to run the personal lives of the staff, who is difficult to approach and has little sense of humour. It may be that the 'constant parent' collects people who are willing to be dependent upon or subordinate to him.

Another type of 'constant parent' is the perpetual nurturer or rescuer who may play the role of benevolent dictator, or she may project as a saintly person who devotes her life to helping others. This person is the continual nurturer who is often drawn into one of the 'helping' professions and may be very effective. Yet, if she keeps others unnecessarily dependent, she is over-indulging her nurturing capacities and does more harm than good.

The person who operates primarily as a 'constant adult' may appear consistently unfeeling, uninvolved and unsympathetic. He is primarily concerned with facts and the processing of information. He may experience trouble on the job if he is in a position which requires supervising others, and is unable to act from the 'nurturing parent' state or joke around from his 'child' state when the situation requires it. The person who operates primarily as a 'constant child' doesn't think for himself, make his own decisions or take responsibility. He may show little conscience in his dealings with others, and is likely to seek out a 'constant parent' to take care of him.

At this stage it will be useful to complete the following 'ego state reaction' quiz to check out understanding of the various ego states.

Ego state reaction quiz
Identify each reaction to the situation as either critical parent CP, nurturing parent NP, adult A, adapted child AC, or natural child NC. (Answers to be found at the end of the chapter on page 91.)

1 A colleague has just been told that he wasn't to get the internal promotion for which he'd applied. You say
    (a) 'Never mind, there will be another chance; it will work out all right in the end'   _____
    (b) 'You think you've been hard done by; have you heard how they treated me?'   _____
    (c) 'You should have gone after it with much more determination'   _____

2 Your boss says 'That new chap in the next department is a right twerp. Still, they are all like that in there'. You say
    (a) 'I haven't really met him yet, so I don't really know'   _____
    (b) 'That's right, it's about time they were sorted out'   _____
    (c) 'Yes, I'm glad you run a better department'   _____

3 After a party in London your spouse says 'Let's go and paddle in the Serpentine'. Your reaction is
   (a) 'What a fun idea; let's go; last one in is a sissy' _____
   (b) 'We shouldn't do that; it's not very dignified' _____
   (c) 'You'll catch a cold, and I'll end up having to coddle you' _____
   (d) 'As long as you don't get too cold and use my scarf to dry your feet afterwards' _____

4 Your secretary arrives late for work for the third time that week. She says
   (a) 'It's not my fault; I did try to get here on time but somehow it didn't work out' _____
   (b) 'It was such a beautiful morning I went for a walk' _____
   (c) 'I do hope that you managed everything OK. Don't worry, I'll soon get things straight for you' _____

5 You have a disagreement with another manager about a policy which is overheard by a colleague, who says
   (a) 'I hope you gave him his come-uppance; I was cheering you on' _____
   (b) 'He should learn to behave himself properly' _____
   (c) 'I couldn't help overhearing. I have a view about it I'd like to discuss with you' _____
   (d) 'Gee, watching it was the best fun I've had all week' _____
   (e) Are you sure you feel OK after that? Let me get you some coffee' _____

6 The lights fuse just when you are about to complete an important report. You say to your secretary
   (a) 'Damn and blast it, I'm going home; to hell with the report' _____
   (b) 'It's about time those maintenance men did a proper job. Just wait until I get hold of the maintenance manager; he ought to do his job' _____
   (c) 'Please 'phone the maintenance department and tell them what's happened' _____

7 Your spouse and you have been to the theatre. On the way home you say
   (a) 'You see, I told you it was too highbrow for you' _____
   (b) 'You didn't enjoy that, did you? It's not fair, you've spoilt the evening for me' _____
   (c) 'I thought the reviews summed it up well' _____
   (d) 'You look tired; shall we get a taxi and go straight home?' _____
(*see* page 91 for answers).

Transactions

A transaction is a communication between two people involving a stimulus and a response from one or more ego states of one person to and from one or more ego states in the other. Transactions can be simple or complex. A conversation consists of a number of ego states linked together. Whenever a person initiates a transaction or responds to one, he has a number of choices as to which ego state he will use and to which ego state of the other person he will direct his communication. There are three kinds of transactions: complementary, crossed and ulterior, each with their own characteristics and rules.

Complementary or parallel transactions

A complementary transaction occurs when a message sent from one ego state gets the expected response from the target ego state in the other person; that is, only two ego states are involved. Here the rule is that *the lines of communication are open and the communication may continue indefinitely.*

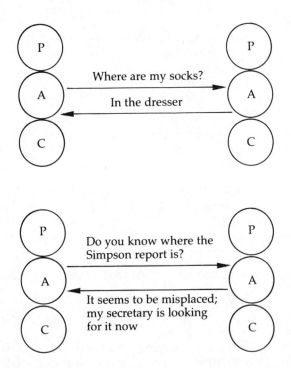

The same initial questions can be asked with a minor change of words, different gestures, tone of voice etc and elicit a different response. For example, a stimulus originating in one person's 'child' ego state frequently brings out the 'parent' ego state in another.

Or it may activate the 'child' in another.

In the particular situation there are a considerable number of combinations that can occur: The distressed 'child' can 'hook in' a nurturing parent, or the critical one, a parent can find another parent, or a 'having fun' child trigger another child. When transactions are complementary communication actually takes place; even though it may not necessarily be constructive at least there is understanding between the parties involved. As long as the response is an expected one the lines of communication remain open and the transaction can continue. An important part of the transaction is the non-verbal aspects as well as the spoken words. Gestures, facial expressions, body posture, tone of voice and so forth all contribute to the meaning.

Crossed transactions
These occur whenever an unexpected response is made from an ego state other than the one to which the stimulus was sent, so that the lines of transactions are crossed. At this point people tend to withdraw, turn away from each other, switch the conversation in another direction or get upset. Crossed transactions are a

frequent source of resentment between people. When two people stand glaring at each other, are unwilling to continue the discussion or are puzzled by what has occured between them it is likely that they have just experienced a crossed transaction.

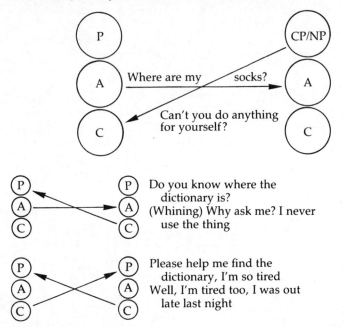

In ordinary social conversation parallel transactions are most often used and the conversation will tend to go on indefinitely. But, there are occasions when it is necessary to try to get someone to change his mind or to prevent oneself being 'hooked' in to an ego state induced by the other person. This can be achieved by effectively crossing the transaction.

An employee says she is sorry but she can't understand why she is always making the same mistake: arriving late for work. She is in her 'adapted child' and hoping to 'hook' a 'nurturing parent' response. It may be necessary for the manager to respond from a different ego state to break off that flow of transaction and so motivate the person to switch ego states. There are any number of options.

Critical parent *Stop putting yourself down and figure out what to do.*
Adult *I know you are capable of sorting the problem out yourself.*
Adapted child *You are making life difficult for me. I wish you'd think of my position.*

Any one of these crossed transactions will break off the original communication and perhaps 'hook' the person into a different kind of response. After the person is in her adult, it is then appropriate to use complementary transactions to reinforce that state. Here the manager may be seen to be operating in his adult ego state, that is, he is understanding what is occurring, but behaving appropriately through some other ego state.

The second rule concerning transactions is that *a crossed transaction will tend to break off the original communication.*

Ulterior transactions

These have a double message, or hidden agenda, so that more than one ego state is involved. This ulterior message is more important to the sender and to the receiver than are the overt, verbal transactions. The convention is to represent ulterior transactions with a dotted line.

If a car salesman says to his customer with a leer, 'This is our finest car, but it may be too fast and expensive for you', he is providing 'adult' information to the prospective buyer. However, he simultaneously sends a secret message to the customer in an attempt to 'hook' his impulsive child and quickly close the deal. The secret message is non-verbal and is the *psychological message*. The adult to adult transaction is overt and is called the *social message*.

If the salesman was successful in 'hooking' the customer's 'child' he may say, 'I'll take it. It's just what I want' from a silent position of 'How dare you say I'm not good enough for this car? I'll show you'.

Such transactions are called angular ones. A duplex transaction involves four ego states, two in each person. During the course of a duplex transaction two conversations are occurring simultaneously, one on the social and another on the psychological level.

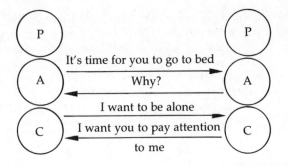

Ulterior messages are the heart of all psychological games. For example, if a woman plays a game of *Rapo*, she baits a man with sexy behaviour ('child' to 'child' ulterior), perhaps while they are discussing a recent news item (plausible 'adult' to 'adult' transaction), then cuts him down when he reaches for the bait. Her message is 'I'm available', even though she has no intention of being available. The pay-off in the game is for her to be able to put the other person down. (Games are explored in more detail shortly.)

The third rule concerning transactions is that *when there is an ulterior element in a transaction it will determine the outcome of the transaction.* Ulterior transactions are not necessarily dishonest but, as has been shown, sometimes secret messages may be used to set people up and obtain negative pay-offs.

Life positions
Right from an early age people develop a view of their own worth and tend to take *life positions* relative to other people. Life positions develop from experiences, particularly those during childhood, and affect the way people feel, act and relate with others. There are four basic life positions, as follows.

I'm OK, you're OK
Persons in this position reflect an optimistic and healthy outlook on life, relate freely with others and assume a 'get on with' stance in their dealings with other persons, the job and life generally. It is potentially a mentally healthy position.

I'm OK, you're not OK
People in this position are often distrusting, blaming or hurting. It is the position of those who put down, victimize or persecute others. They blame others for their problems and express hostility or anger. Some extremely ambitious people take this position (I'll

climb over everyone to get to the top) as do the zealots and bigots (mine is the right way, the only way).

I'm not OK, you're OK
This is a common position of persons who feel powerless when they compare themselves with others, and they tend to withdraw or experience depression. Persons in this position often feel stupid, inferior, ugly or inadequate. As distrust of others may also accompany this position, such people may have great difficulty in accepting compliments and in their dealings with others.

I'm not OK, you're not OK
This is the position of people who have decided that neither themselves nor anyone else is worthwhile and valuable, and who lose interest in living. These persons generally assume 'a get nowhere with' stance in their dealings with other persons.

Strokes
It is well established that infants need physical contact in order to survive and grow. As people grow from childhood to adults the need for 'strokes' continues and becomes, at least in part, a need for recognition. Since physical touching among adults is less acceptable in our society, words, smiles, nods, frowns, gestures etc tend to be used instead. The rule seems to be that negative strokes are better than no strokes at all, although it is positive strokes that nourish a person.

A positive stroke is one which carries a 'you're OK' message and usually results in the recipient feeling good, alive, alert and significant. A negative stroke is one which carries a 'you're not OK' message and results in unpleasant feelings. The pattern of stroking, given, refused or received, tends to reflect the life position a person is in. People who feel OK about themselves and others tend to seek out exchanges of positive strokes; those who feel others are not OK tend to give negative strokes, and those who feel I'm not OK tend to seek out negative strokes which will increase their not OK feelings. To receive negative strokes is better than receiving no strokes at all and may serve to confirm a person's favourite and comfortable view of himself (I'm not OK). All forms of stroking recognize the existence of an individual. The worst situation is to receive no stroking at all, as in this way an individual's existence is denied. Strokes may be conditional (for doing) or unconditional (for being) as follows:

+ ve, unconditional   I like you
+ ve, conditional   I'll like you if you do this for me

– ve, conditional	I'll shout at you if you do that
– ve, unconditional	I'll shout at you anyway

Conditional strokes, both positive and negative, are often used to modify other people's behaviour. To use an illustration away from a work setting, a mother may give a child positive, conditional strokes when the child uses the toilet and negative ones when he wets the floor.

People collect the feelings, both good and bad, that they receive from stroking by others, and eventually 'cash' them in when the collection is sufficiently large. Have you ever seen a 'put down' collected and passed down a chain of command? For example, a manager may receive some negative strokes from his wife before leaving for work in the morning. No resolution of the problem is made: he collects the bad feelings and carries them off with him. He cashes them in on one of his supervisors with, 'What's the matter with you? I expected this report at 9 am not 10 am'. The supervisor collects bad feelings and takes them back to his secretary to cash in. 'Didn't you see that note I left? Why can't you get things to me on time? I also found several typing errors in that last report'. The secretary goes home and cashes in on her husband. 'The house looks a mess as usual; it's about time you realized that I'm not a servant to clear up after you'. The husband turns to the children with, 'It's your fault. Look at the stuff you've left around for us to stumble over'. The children may cash in by kicking the dog.

People acquire bad feeling collections of different sizes before discharging them. Some turn in relatively small collections for small prizes: having a headache, dressing down an employee etc. Others save up a bigger collection and obtain bigger negative prizes. When a person feels he has collected enough negative feelings and is ready to discharge them certain phrases are often used to indicate redemption time is at hand:

> 'That's the last straw'
> 'I've taken all I'm going to'
> 'I've had it up to here'

There are some jobs, reception clerk, air hostess, sales representative are examples, where the holders are often the recipient of the cashing in of bad feelings. Here the particular mishap that provokes the outburst is rarely sufficient to justify the strength of feeling expressed. Rather, the mishap provides an opportunity for the discharge of an accumulation of bad feelings. Training in transactional analysis has sometimes been used to enable staff to handle such a situation. Generally the rule here is to stay in one's adult state and not to let the child or critical parent become 'hooked' in.

Games

People sometimes play psychological games of which they are often unaware, and may relate to those people who will play the role opposite their own. Such games tend to be repetitious, and a manager can come to recognize which games are being played by whom and how to deal with them. Importantly she should also come to recognize the games that she tends to play with others.

Although there are many different games in each one there are three basic elements:

1 a series of complementary transactions which on the surface seem plausible
2 an ulterior transaction which represents the hidden agenda
3 a negative pay-off which concludes the game and is the real purpose for playing.

People play games with different degrees of intensity: some may be no more than gentle teasing while others may be more, such as deliberately setting someone up so he can be slapped down.

Even as some people have favourite ego states, they also have a favourite game role which either serves to reinforce a negative position about others—you're not OK (you need to be punished or rescued)—or to reinforce a negative position about oneself—I'm not OK (I need you to punish me or rescue me). Games prevent honest and open relationships between the players. Yet people play them because they fill up time, provoke attention, provide a way of getting and giving strokes, and fulfil a sense of identity and destiny. Some common games are:

Yes, but

A person who plays 'yes, but' does so to maintain a position of 'nobody's going to tell me what to do' or 'people are stupid'. One player presents a problem in the guise of soliciting advice from one or more other players.

If 'hooked' the other player advises 'why don't you. . . .?' The initiator discounts all suggestions with 'yes, but . . .', followed by 'reasons' why the advice won't work. Eventually the 'why don't you' advice-givers give up and fall silent and maybe get uncomfortable, frustrated, depressed. This is the pay-off of the game.

Kick me

In a game of 'kick me' the player does something to provoke another player to put him down. Though he may deny it, a person who sets up the game of 'kick me' tends to attract others who can play the complementary hand and are willing to 'kick' him.

Harried

Harried is a common game. An executive who plays 'harried' says 'yes' to everything, volunteers to come early and work late, takes on week-end assignments and carries work home in a briefcase—perhaps even studying it on the bus. For a period he is able to act like superman but eventually his appearance begins to reflect his harried state, and he is able to cash in on his favourite feeling of feeling depressed and put upon.

Blemish

You're fine except for a minor blemish—length of hair, style of clothes etc, which really spoils everything.

I'm only trying to help you

My advice is so good, why do you want to think for yourself and reject my ideas when I'm only trying to help you?

Wooden leg

Surely you can't expect much from me when I have such a handicap, ie wrong sex, wrong size, wrong race, wrong background etc.

See how hard I tried

Don't blame me if things turn out wrong. After all, see how hard I tried. The game is to 'try' but not to achieve.

Uproar

I'm stronger than you are. You stupid fool, you never do anything right.

Now I've got you

I've caught you making a mistake and will now make you suffer.

Let you and him fight

I wouldn't stand for that if I were you; I'd go and tell him what you think.

Dealing with games

The primary rule in dealing with games players is of course to recognize that a game is being played and to refuse to become 'hooked' into it. In such interpersonal transactions a manager may become bewildered, anxious or hurt unless he recognizes what is going on, and it is important to respond from the adult ego state in such situations. Games may be foiled by a refusal to play the expected hand (replying with a crossed transaction) or a refusal to give a pay-off. For example, refusing to give advice or suggestions to a *Yes, But* player usually stops the game. Of course it may be that the reason a manager's interpersonal relationships are poor is because she is playing games with others!

Summary
Transactional analysis is a useful way for a manager to examine relationships and interactions with others. As was stressed earlier, it has not been the intention to encourage you to psychoanalyse others: to put on a clinician's white coat, so to speak. Rather, if you can identify behaviours and have some clues into possible reasons for them TA can be of great benefit.

This applies equally to you yourself, not just the person you are interacting with. Difficulties in relationships with others may stem primarily from you: your view of the world, the appropriateness of the ego state you act from for particular situations, your life position, your skill in transacting with others, etc. Before you can become aware of and sensitive to the behaviours and ego states of others you must be aware of and sensitive to your own.

From this can come greater skill and awareness, using complementary or crossed transactions where appropriate. You can prevent yourself becoming 'hooked' into unproductive transactions and games, and thus avoid feelings of bewilderment, anxiety or hurt. Above all you can improve your effectiveness.

Activity plans

Activity 1
In chapter 2 you rated the leadership style you perceived yourself having across three dimensions. Ask your boss, some of the people who report to you and some colleagues to rate your style using the same dimensions. Are there any differences in perceptions and, if so, how large are these? What are the consequences for feedback and self awareness?

Activity 2
Draw an egograph for yourself as you perceive yourself for most of the time (a) at work, (b) at home. Do you have a favourite ego state for these two situations? Are you satisfied with this? How could you become more effective in your relationships?

Activity 3

Stroke profile
Shade in the following profile. Take time to reflect quietly on your work life and your personal (ie non-work) life and experiences.

		RECEIVE		GIVE		ASK FOR		REFUSE	
		Personal	Work	Personal	Work	Personal	Work	Personal	Work
POS	always								
	usually								
	often								
	sometimes								
	almost never								
NEG	almost never								
	sometimes								
	often								
	usually								
	always								

A *positive stroke* is one which carries a 'you're OK' message and usually results in the recipient feeling good, alive, alert and significant,

    eg You do look good today

        What a splendid idea.

A *negative stroke* is one which carries a 'you're not OK' message and results in unpleasant feelings,

    eg You made a fool of yourself, acting like that

        You should have worn different coloured shoes with that dress.

Activity 4

Think of the last two occasions on which a discussion you had went badly wrong. Analyse what happened in terms of ego states and transactions. How could the discussion have been better handled?

Activity 5

Recall a recent situation in which you collected and held negative feelings. What type of feelings were these, how and on whom were they cashed in? Could you have handled the situation a different way so you didn't collect bad feelings?

Answers to ego state reaction quiz on page 78

1 (a) NP (b) AC (c) CP   2 (a) A (b) CP (c) AC
3 (a) NC (b)CP (c) AC (d) NP   4 (a) AC (b) NC (c) NP
5 (a) AC (b) CP (c) A (d) NC (e) NP   6 (a) NC (b) CP (c) A
7 (a) CP (b) AC (c) A (d) NP
(It is possible that some words can indicate different ego states, depending on the tone of voice and context of the remark.)

6 Making a difference: personal power and influence

The core purpose in any management activity is to make a difference, to shape and influence events. Management is not a passive role, or one concerned with being, it involves proactivity and the results come from doing. A manager's degree of expertise matters not if he or she cannot influence events and people, or have an impact on what to achieve and how to achieve it. This particularly applies where people are involved, whether they be peers, subordinates or seniors.

There is an old Romanian curse which says 'May you have a brilliant idea which you know is right and be unable to convince others'.

To influence people and events requires a degree of personal power. Personal power is different from mere authority. As described in Chapter 1 authority may come from structural position in the hierarchy, or be based on expertise, personal or moral qualities. Increasingly people are finding themselves in rôles which require personal power—a set of skills, attitudes, energies and behaviours—in order to get things done, and where the possession of structural power is no longer sufficient. Some common examples include project managers, staff people and consultants. Even in line positions the exercise of structural authority without personal power is unlikely to produce the quality of action required. More and more, managers are required to be 'animateurs', not 'amateurs'.

Equally, expertise is of itself insufficient; it is the application of that expertise into action, through other people, that matters, in other words how that personal power is used to influence other people and events.

Power and influence are two highly charged words, having

particular connotations for certain people. It is useful to distinguish between the two faces of power and influence, its positive aspect and its negative side. Positive power accomplishes the objective by working with and through others without damaging or weakening them, while negative power weakens and diminishes others and their personal power. In the long term negative power tends to be less effective than positive, because of the impoverishment of people, the conflict it engenders and other unintended consequences. Equally, the use of positive power tends to empower others, be enriching, and leads to better quality decisions. Positive power implies a win-win while the use of negative power often results in win-lose or lose-lose situations. People who are basically strong, and have personal positive power tend to use positive power, whereas often less secure and able people tend to rely on the negative kind.

Further, in the context of management, it is important to make a difference through people by exercising personal power and influence. Interestingly this is equally so outside the world of work, whether it be in the home or with relationships generally. Personal power has much to do with being aware of our wants and needs as they occur and taking personal responsibility, through exercising a wide range of choices, for getting them met or not. This can be visualized as shown below.

Figure 26
The need satisfaction and influence cycle

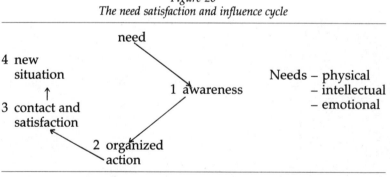

1st stage – being aware of the need (particularly those based on our feelings)

2nd stage – taking action to get the need satisfied. This involves exercising as wide a range of choices in influencing as possible

3rd stage – making contact with the other individual and achieving satisfaction

4th stage – new situation. As the need/want is satisfied another emerges

People can go through the cycle in a matter of moments and achieve satisfaction and a sense of self-worth; however, some people continually fall into old patterns of behaviour that sabotage their ability to get what they want.

How people give away their personal power

1 Limiting their range of choices in influencing others. They do this by either punishing themselves for past behaviours which have, in their terms, been unsuccessful or fantasizing about what might happen if they exercised a particular choice in dealing with someone, eg if I say 'no', he/she will never talk to me again.
2 Ignoring, denying, or repressing their own feelings as a basis for recognizing and getting what is wanted. In effect, people turn their feelings inwards, thus stopping themselves making contact with others, eg getting angry with themselves rather than others.
3 Swallowing down whole rules, standards, beliefs about themselves and how they are to interact with others without questioning their appropriateness to their everyday life. These values then become barriers to building effective relationships—

   —I must not trust others
   —I must always be polite
   —Never show your feelings

4 Avoiding responsibility, minimizing or denying the importance of the need or situation, eg

   'My career is the company's responsibility, not mine.'

   'My career is not important, compared with other issues the company has to consider.'

In summary personal power and influence is a key factor in management and in our lives generally. It can be used positively, with much effect, or negatively with possible short-term benefits but negative longer-term ones. Personal power is inextricably linked with leadership. It may be we have doubts about people who seek power and influence, because we fear that they may be seeking power and influence in order to exploit us. Equally, as managers we may have our own doubts about exercising leadership, because we may fear that others may regard us as persons who seek power and influence in order to exploit. What is being described here is not causing submission and dependency, which is one aspect of the employment of negative power, but the positive power to empower other people to be able to achieve their goals, to take responsibility and to make commitment to action.

94

Influencing styles

In all this it is important to have a sufficient range of influencing skills to deal with different situations. One common concern about the use of power and influence is that it can lead to conflict, this again will be explored shortly, but it is worth saying at this stage that conflict is not necessarily bad, it can result in highly productive outcomes—it is the way such conflict is resolved that matters.

Influencing is the process of modifying, effecting or changing someone else's behaviour, attitudes or thoughts. There are a number of influencing styles, each with its own advantages and disadvantages, with the success of each depending upon the situation, so some flexibility is required. This chapter concentrates on Assertion, which is a particularly direct form of exercising personal power. Assertion training is also a very useful way for empowering people and developing their self-confidence.

Assertion

Assertiveness is standing up for oneself and one's rights in such a way that the other person's rights are not violated, and that other person is not 'put down'. It involves being aware of and responsive to the rights and resources of others without denying or limiting one's own rights and resources. It is thus a form of positive personal power, expressed more as a 'push' than 'pull' and differs significantly from Aggression which is a form of negative personal power. Aggression is concerned with standing up for oneself and one's rights in such a way that the rights of others are violated in the process. Non-assertive behaviour is to fail to stand up for oneself and one's rights effectively, and is an expression of powerlessness. The three basic styles are shown diagrammatically below.

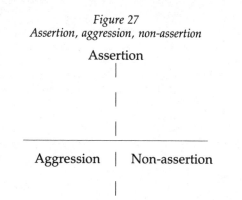

Figure 27
Assertion, aggression, non-assertion

Assertion

Aggression | Non-assertion

Suppose a co-worker keeps giving you all of his/her work to do. You decide to put an end to this. The person has just asked you to do some more of his/her work.

Assertion

An assertive response in this situation could be 'No [name] I'm not going to do any more of your work. I have decided that it's not right for either of us for me to do both my work and yours.'

So assertiveness is based upon the beliefs that, in any situation, you have needs to be met and so do the other people involved: you have rights; so do the others: you have something to contribute and so do others.

Aggression

An aggressive response to this situation could be 'Forget it. It's about time you did it. You treat me like your slave. You're an inconsiderate s.o.b.'

Aggressive behaviour is based on the belief that your needs, wants and opinions are more important than other people's: you have rights but other people don't; you have something to contribute, others have little or nothing.

The aim of aggression is to win, if necessary at the expense of others.

Non-assertion

A non-assertive response to the situation could be 'I'm rather busy. But if you can't get it done I think I can help you.'

So non-assertion is based upon the belief that, in any situation, the other person's needs and wants are more important than yours; the other person has rights, but you have very few; you have little to contribute whereas the other person has a great deal.

Typically, non-assertion is used to avoid conflict and to please or placate others.

Below is another example illustrating the three different behaviours being used to handle the same situation.

Situation

Taking back an unsatisfactory letter to the person who prepared it.

Assertion

'Frances, I'd like you to re-do this letter as there are several mistakes in it.'

96

Aggression
'I don't know how you can give me this kind of stuff. It's full of mistakes.'

Non-assertion
You may find an excuse not to take the letter back, or you say something like 'I know its probably my fault, Ann, not writing very clearly but is there any chance you could get some time to change just one or two things?'

To summarize then, the basic stance taken, the underlying intention and beliefs, the behaviour characteristics and effect on others are as follows for the three modes:

Assertive

Basic stance
To stand up for oneself and one's rights in such a way that the other person's rights are not violated.

Intention
To communicate, to influence others, to use one's resources, and to gain self-respect without diminishing others. To find out *what* is right, not who is right.

Belief
I Win/You Win. I'm OK. We are both responsible. I have rights. I value my resources.

Behaviour characteristics
Expressive, descriptive, firm but not hostile. 'I' messages are clear: willing to give information, express goals and expectations, and may 'sell'.

Effect on others
Others feel in touch, informed, enhanced. They can disagree without being seen as attackers or being judged incompetent. Their contributions and influence often increase.

Aggressive

Basic stance
To stand up for oneself and one's rights in such a way that the rights of others *are* violated in the process.

Intention
To be 'on top', put others down. Self-enhancing at the expense of the other. To influence outcomes without being influenced.

Belief
I Win/You Lose. I'm OK—You're not OK. Victim feeling: I'll get you before you get me. 'You have no right . . .'. Your resources are limited. 'Top dog' is the only safe position. I am right.

Behaviour characteristics
Towards others: dominating, overpowering, accusatory, contemptuous, condescending, degrading and attacking. Self-orientated.

Effect on others
Others feel hurt, defensive, humiliated, fearful, resentful, underutilized, dependent. They can't disagree without being seen as either presumptuous, defensive, or incompetent.

Non-assertive
Basic stance
To fail to stand up for oneself and one's rights effectively.

Intention
To be 'safe', to appease, to let others take responsibility, to rely on the resources of others, to get help or sympathy, to deny one's own needs, interests and resources.

Belief
I Lose/You Win. I'm not OK—You're OK. Victim feeling: You'll get me if I'm not 'nice'. 'I have no right . . .'. 'Bottom dog' is the only safe position. I have limited resources. I can't contribute much.

Behaviour characteristics
Whining, apologetic, 'hurt feelings', passive (but harbours bad feeling). Self-orientated behaviour, puts self down while placing blame on others (eg 'I'm not very good at this but I might have succeeded if you had only given me more help'). Overly agreeable, goes along.

98

Effect on others
Others feel guilty, frustrated, angry or shackled. They can't disagree without 'hurting' or being seen as unconcerned or hostile toward the non-assertive individual.

Assertion is expressed of course through verbal and non-verbal behaviour. The words can be assertive, but the 'music', that is the non-verbal aspects, need to be congruent with the words. For example, three kinds of non-verbals can accompany the statement 'I don't want to do that':

—using a soft, whining voice, looking away and wringing one's hands
—using a strong, steadying tone, standing comfortably and erect and looking at the other person
—speaking in a raised or aggrieved tone
—leaning towards the other person, pointing and glaring at him

The same message can be made to appear non-assertive, assertive or aggressive by differing non-verbals.

Equally, the words used may not support an assertive non-verbal stance. One example of this particularly is the use of 'qualifiers'—words or phrases that discount the immediacy of the message:

—'I hope you don't mind, but'
—'I may be wrong, but'

The word 'but' is a very common qualifier which dilutes the effect of the message. Others include:

—'just' ('I just wanted to explore this')
—'kind of', 'sort of' ('I kind of think it's wrong') ('I was—sort of—unhappy about what you said')
—'little' ('There is a little issue I need to raise')
—'sorry' ('I'm sorry to bring this up')

and hesitating and minimizing generally.

Behaviours
A summary of some of the aspects of behaviour that distinguish assertive from aggressive and non-assertive behaviour is shown overleaf.

When you have become familiar with these, it will be useful to complete the following exercise questionnaire on recognizing assertive, aggressive and non-assertive behaviour. The next stage is to practise assertiveness and some exercises for this are given at the end of the chapter.

Non-assertive	Assertive	Aggressive
—Long, rambling statements —Fill-in words: 'maybe' —Frequent justifications —Apologies and 'permission seekers' —'I should', 'I ought' —Few 'I' statements (often qualified) —Phrases that dismiss own needs: 'not important really' —Self put-downs 'I'm hopeless'	—Statements that are brief, clear and to the point —'I' statements: 'I'd like' —Distinctions between fact and opinion —Suggestions not weighted with 'advice' —No 'shoulds' nor 'oughts' —Constructive 'criticism' without blame or assumptions —Questions to find out the thoughts, opinions, wants of others —Ways of getting round problems	—Excess of 'I' statements —Boastfulness, 'My' —Opinions expressed as facts —Threatening questions —Requests as instructions or threats —Heavily weighted advice in the form of 'should' and 'ought' —Blame put on others —Assumptions —Sarcasm and other put-downs

Activity plan 1

Questionnaire: recognizing assertive, non-assertive and aggressive behaviour. You identify which is which for each of the ten questions.

1   A colleague rings when you are working on a project that you particularly want to finish. He says he wants to talk about next week's meeting. You prefer to discuss the matter later.

'I'm happy to talk about the meeting, but right now I want to finish this project. I'll ring you back this afternoon.'   ☐

'I'm busy. It's always the same, I can't get work done because of pointless interruptions.'   ☐

'Well, I am busy, but I guess I can find time now if it's important to you.'   ☐

2   Your friend has just arrived an hour late for dinner and did not call you to let you know. You are annoyed about this.

    'Shall we sit down and start?'   ☐

    'I've been waiting an hour. I would have appreciated it if you had called me.'   ☐

    'Where the hell have you been? What a mess. I'm not going to invite you again.'   ☐

3   An article you bought yesterday is faulty. You want it replaced not repaired.

    'This is a load of rubbish. Give me another one and make sure it works this time. I won't shop here again in a hurry.'   ☐

    'I bought this from you yesterday. It's faulty and I want it replaced.'   ☐

    'Would you mind, if it's not too much trouble, looking at this for me. It may not be quite right.'   ☐

4   A colleague compliments you for a piece of work.

    'Thank you.'   ☐

    'It's nothing really.'   ☐

    'What do you expect from me, I only do excellent work.'   ☐

5   You're out with a group of friends. You're all deciding which film to see. One person has just mentioned a film you don't want to see.

    'That one's rubbish. No one in his right mind would want to see that.'   ☐

    'Well, I'll go along if that's what everyone else wants.'   ☐

    'I don't want to see that one. How about the one at the Rialto?'   ☐

6   Your boss has just criticized one of your staff. You feel the criticism unjustified.

    'I feel your criticism is unfair. He/she is not like that at all.'   ☐

'I'm the manager, and I know him/her best. You should trust me to deal with my own people.' □

'I hadn't thought about it but I suppose you are right.' □

7   Your friends call and say they are coming to visit tonight. You already have plans for the evening which you don't want to break.

'No. I'm busy. You take me for granted. I do have a life of my own.' □

'I can't make it tonight, I already have plans for the evening. Call me again.' □

'Well, I suppose so, but I was doing something else.' □

8   One of your staff deserves a low assessment because of continued poor performance that has been discussed previously.

'Look, the company requires me to rate your performance. It's very difficult for me. What problems have you had that affect your performance?' □

'I'm disappointed that your performance has not improved since the last appraisal. Let's try to get things sorted once and for all this time, so you can do well.' □

'You never learn, do you. It's time you got yourself sorted out. You are for the high jump this review.' □

9   Your spouse switches TV channels when you are part-way through watching a programme that interests you.

'You are always doing that. It's rude and boring. You are an inconsiderate so and so. Turn it back over, now!' □

'I'm annoyed that you switched off a programme without consulting me. I was interested in the programme and want to finish it.' ☐

'What is it you would like to watch, is it important?' ☐

10 Your company operates a flexi-hours system. You require one of your people to work a schedule that means he/she is required to work for slightly different hours for one week. The flexi-hours regulations allow this but the person has got into the habit of catching a particular bus.

'I want you to work this schedule for next week. It's necessary to meet the needs for the job, which must take priority. I'll explore with you any reasonable ways of overcoming any problems.' ☐

'Would you mind helping me out with a spot of bother. It's difficult for me. You see the company wants this schedule worked next week. It's inconvenient for you, I know, but I hope it's not too inconvenient.' ☐

'You get paid to do the work the company sets. This is your schedule for next week. I don't want to hear any argument about it.' ☐

Question

1	assertive	aggressive	non-assertive
2	non-assertive	assertive	aggressive
3	aggressive	assertive	non-assertive
4	assertive	non-assertive	aggressive
5	aggressive	non-assertive	assertive
6	assertive	aggressive	non-assertive
7	aggressive	assertive	non-assertive
8	non-assertive	assertive	aggressive
9	aggressive	assertive	non-assertive
10	assertive	non-assertive	aggressive

The assertion model provides a simple and powerful way of developing one set of influencing skills, and reducing undesired behaviours such as aggression and non-assertion with their negative consequences. It is readily trainable, particularly if some of the techniques to be described are used. It lends itself to a set of

103

learned responses, following the well-known path from being—

unconsciously incompetent	—where lack of skill and its effect is not recognized
to consciously incompetent	—being aware of lack of skills
to consciously competent	—having the skills but using them consciously
to unconsciously competent	—having the skills and using them unconsciously and without embarrassment

Like all models of behaviour, there is no one uniform style or approach that is right for all situations. In situations of self-survival, for example, an aggressive response might be sometimes appropriate; equally the non-assertive stance may be appropriate where there are, for example, legal or moral issues involved with which the person is not sufficiently familiar. For the vast majority of situations, though, within the context of this model, a form of assertive behaviour is likely to be most appropriate.

One of the common fallacies that many people who habitually operate from a non-assertive stance have is that they will be disliked, or cause offence, if they speak their minds, that is to say they will become aggressive. It is also a position of low self-confidence, regard and self-respect. Typically, non-assertion, when assertion is called for, induces feelings of negativeness, which are internalized as fear, guilt, anxiety, depression or whatever, and can result in a sudden switch to aggression. Self-confidence, or the lack of it, is often associated with non-assertive behaviour and, equally, a movement to more assertion reinforces feelings of self-confidence.

Activity plan 2

Personal power exercises
1 Think of the last time you chose to repress a strong feeling.
  (a) What were the immediate consequences?
    —for self (eg agitation, confusion, etc)
    —for others (eg uncertainty, hostility, etc)
  (b) What were the long-term consequences?
    —for self (eg distraction, regret, etc)
    —for others (eg distrust, disbelief, etc)
  (c) On reflection what do you imagine could have happened if you had expressed the feeling at the time?
    —good consequences
    —bad consequences

2 Think of a time when you felt and acted powerfully.

(a) Was it positive personal power or negative you were feeling?
(b) How did you behave?
(c) What did it feel like (i) at the time, (ii) afterwards?
(d) What were the consequences and results, including the effects on other people?

3 Now repeat the exercise for an occasion when you displayed
   (a) the opposite kind of power to that considered above
   (b) feelings of powerlessness

What are your conclusions?

Influence exercises

Individual

1 Identify one person at work who is important to you in some way (work together often; a friend; someone you are in conflict with, etc). This person may be a boss, a peer or a subordinate.

2 Reflect on your relationship with that person:
   (a) what words would you use to describe your behaviour?
   (b) what words would you use to describe his/her behaviour?
   (c) what feelings do you have? what feelings do you know or assume that the other person has in the relationship?

3 Reviewing the above answers how do you influence each other?

Small group

1 In small groups take it in turns to share your answers to the above questions.

2 (a) based on your discussions what have you discovered about influencing?
   (b) what are the key skills of influencing?

Assertion exercises

1 Each person writes down their answers to the following questions:
   (a) What natural abilities do I have?
   (b) What thing do I do better than most people?
   (c) The most difficult things I have accomplished in my life?
   (d) What am I most proud of?
   (20 minutes)

2 In small groups of four, each person takes it in turn to read out their answers.

Speaker, pay attention to their feelings.
Listeners, pay attention to non-verbal behaviours.
(30 minutes)

3 In full groups discuss the experience.

4 Think of a situation that you find difficult to handle and which bothers you. You may have been putting off dealing with it for some time. Write a short script on what you wanted to say, using an assertive approach. Refine and practise the script. Deal with the situation. Review how it went and how you felt about it.

5 There are many everyday situations in which to practise assertion. Examples of these are given below. Make a point of using these opportunities, not artificially but in a real sense, for developing your feelings of positive personal power and your skill in asserting.

—telling someone the things you would like them to do more often
—obtaining a better table in a restaurant
—returning unacceptable goods
—getting something loaned returned
—asking for a raise
—refusing a request
—telling someone that he/she is doing something that bothers or offends you, eg smoking

7 Handling interpersonal conflict

This chapter looks at the appropriateness of different choices available when in conflict with others. After a self-assessment activity plan, ways of handling different types of conflict are examined.

Managing conflict situations
Conflict situations are those where the concerns of two or more people appear to be incompatible. Such situations may need to be resolved by a manager when other people or groups are involved, or he may be part of that conflict, that is be one of the parties involved. Conflict may be manifested in all kinds of ways—criticism, anger, sarcasm, aggression, fear, tears, apathy, blocking, low performance, etc—but ways largely connected to feelings and emotions. Its causes, though, are more to do with factors such as needs, interests, rôles, pressures, personality, resources, lack of awareness and skills. This introduces the first rule about conflict management, that is that the conflict is only likely to be well resolved when the level of feelings and emotion connected with it is dealt with sufficiently so that the underlying causes can be addressed.

Conflict is not necessarily bad; from it can come some very productive outcomes. It is also a part of everyday life, where competition for resources, alternative demands, differing view-points give rise to the potential for better quality decisions and outcomes, or alternatively the playing of the zero sum game. This is where one party 'loses' all as a result of the other party 'winning'.

There are a number of sayings in the language of our conventional wisdom that refer to the management of conflict. They include 'Might is right', 'Leave well enough alone', 'Two hands are better than one', 'Split the difference' and 'Kill your enemies with kindness'. It may be seen that all of these might have some value in resolving conflict; the effectiveness of any one approach depends on the requirements of the specific conflict situation. In other words, like management style generally, what is appropriate depends on the situation.

Equally, as people we tend to have a number of biases or orientations towards conflict resolution so that we tend to react in predisposed ways. Although we may not rely on a single rigid style, as individuals we may tend to use some styles better than others and therefore, whether because of temperament, skills or habit, will tend to rely on those styles more readily than others.

The effectiveness of conflict handling then depends upon the given situation and the method best suited for resolving it, and the orientations and skills with which the particular style is used.

Conflict handling styles
Shortly, a model which looks at different approaches to handling conflict will be explored, together with the options available for handling it. As a first step, however, it would be useful to use the following questionnaire to help identify your approach to conflict.

Activity plan 1
Individual approaches to conflict: questionnaire
This is intended to help you clarify the way you approach and attempt to resolve conflict. From each of the paired statements below, choose one which best fits your preferred approach:

1.1 Differences of opinion often don't matter a great deal.
  2 Usually I am single-minded in achieving my aims.
2.1 If there is a disagreement I like to win.
  2. I prefer not to spend much time with individuals who voice strong opinions.
3.1 I prefer to stick with my own ideas rather than enter a long discussion.
  2 When I have made up my mind I try hard to convince others.
4.1 If there is a problem I like both sides to put their cards on the table.
  2 Differences of opinion often don't matter a great deal.
5.1 I prefer not to spend much time with individuals who voice strong opinions.
  2 I like to be very open and encourage others to be the same.
6.1 It is better to explore agreement rather than disagreement.
  2 I prefer to stick with my own ideas rather than enter a long discussion.

7.1 If there is a problem I like both sides to put their cards on the table.

2 I usually prefer to share the cake rather than try to get it all.

8.1 I like to be very open and encourage others to be the same.

2 It is better to arrive at a settlement where everybody gets something, rather than stick out to get most advantage for myself.

9.1 It is better to explore agreement rather than disagreement.

2 In a dispute both sides need to make significant concessions.

10.1 Sometimes I give others what they want, even when I would rather not.

2 If there is a problem I like both sides to put their cards on the table.

11.1 I like to be very open and encourage others to be the same.

2 It is often better to accept another's viewpoint rather than antagonize them.

12.1 Often it is best to follow other people's ideas.

2 It is better to explore agreement rather than disagreement.

13.1 Usually I am single-minded in achieving my aims.

2 If there is a problem I like both sides to put their cards on the table.

14.1 I like to be very open and encourage others to be the same.

2 If there is a disagreement, I like to win.

15.1 When I have made up my mind I try hard to convince others.

2 It is better to explore agreement rather than disagreement.

16.1 Sometimes I give others what they want, even when I would rather not.

2 Differences of opinion don't often matter a great deal.

17.1 It is often better to accept another's viewpoint rather than antagonize them.

2 I prefer not to spend much time with individuals who voice strong opinions.

18.1 Often it is best to follow other people's ideas.

2 I prefer to stick with my own ideas rather than enter a long discussion.

19.1 I usually prefer to share the cake rather than try to get it all.

2 Usually I am single-minded in achieving my aims.

20.1 If there is a disagreement I like to win.

2 It is better to arrive at a settlement where everybody gets something, rather than stick out to get most advantage for myself.

22.1 Differences of opinion often don't matter a great deal.

2 When I have made up my mind I try hard to convince others.

22.1 Differences of opinion often don't matter a great deal.

2 I usually prefer to share the cake rather than try to get it all.

23.1 It is better to arrive at a settlement where everybody gets

something, rather than stick out to get most advantage for myself.
   2 I prefer not to spend much time with individuals who voice strong opinions.
24.1 I prefer to stick with my own ideas rather than enter a long discussion.
   2 In a dispute both sides need to make significant concessions.
25.1 Usually I am single-minded in achieving my aims.
   2 Sometimes I give others what they want, even when I would rather not.
26.1 It is often better to accept another's viewpoint rather than antagonize them.
   2 If there is a disagreement I like to win.
27.1 When I have made up my mind I try hard to convince others.
   2 Often it is best to follow other people's ideas.
28.1 I usually prefer to share the cake rather than try to get it all.
   2 Sometimes I give others what they want, even when I would rather not.
29.1 It is often better to accept another's viewpoint rather than antagonize them.
   2 It is better to arrive at a settlement where everybody gets something, rather than stick out to get most advantage for myself.
30.1 In a dispute both sides need to make significant concessions.
   2 Often it is best to follow other people's ideas.

Approaches to conflict: scoring key

The questionnaire consists of three statements reflecting each of the five conflict-handling styles:

   avoiding
   accommodating
   compromising
   competing
   collaborating

Each statement is paired in comparison with one statement from each of the other four approaches. The key opposite indicates to you how to score the questionnaire. If you chose the first statement of the first pair then you would score 1 for avoiding. If you chose the first statement of the second pair you would score 1 for competing and so on. The maximum score for any approach is 12 and the total score is 30. A score of more than 6 on any approach would indicate a preference for that approach, while a score of less than 6 would indicate that it is not preferred. This is not a 'scientific' instrument revealing the 'truths' about you! It should only be used

110

in conjunction with other evidence which you have about your approach to conflict. Put a circle round your choice, then add up the figures circled in each column.

STATEMENT PAIR	CONFLICT RESOLUTION STYLE				
	AVOID	ACCOMMODATE	COMPROMISE	COMPETE	COLLABORATE
1	1			2	
2	2			1	
3	1			2	
4	2				1
5	1				2
6	2				1
7			2		1
8			2		1
9			2		1
10		1			2
11		2			1
12		1			2
13				1	2
14				2	1
15				1	2
16	2	1			
17	2	1			
18	2	1			
19			1	2	
20			2	1	
21			1	2	
22	1		2		
23	2		1		
24	1		2		
25		2		1	
26		1		2	
27		2		1	
28		2	1		
29		1	2		
30		2	1		
TOTALS					

The Thomas-Kilman conflict handling model
In this model a person's behaviour when dealing with conflict situations is described along two basic dimensions:

1 Assertiveness, the extent to which the individual attempts to satisfy her own concerns, and
2 Co-operativeness, the extent to which the individual attempts to satisfy the other person's concerns

It should be noted that assertiveness as used here is not defined in precisely the same way as used earlier in the book. Here the assertive dimension in conjunction with the unco-operative one (Competing) results in a situation similar to that defined earlier as aggression.

The five basic styles or modes in the Thomas-Kilman model are shown below.

Figure 28
Handling conflict

CO-OPERATIVE

ACCOMMODATING: neglecting one's own concerns to satisfy those of the other party, eg
—selfless generosity or charity
—accepting an instruction when one would prefer not to
—yielding to another's point of view

COLLABORATING: working with the other party to find some solution which fully satisfies the concerns of both parties, eg
—exploring disagreements to learn from each other
—concluding to resolve a condition which would otherwise lead to competition over resources
—confronting and finding a creative solution to an interpersonal problem

UNASSERTIVE ——————

COMPROMISING: finding an expedient, mutually acceptable solution, partially satisfying both parties, eg
—'splitting the difference'
—'exchanging concessions'

—————— ASSERTIVE

AVOIDING: not pursuing one's own concerns *or* those of the other party. Not addressing the conflict, eg
—diplomatically sidestepping an issue
—postponing an issue until a better time
—withdrawing from a threatening situation

COMPETING: pursuing one's own concerns at the expense of the other party, using ability to argue, status, economic sanctions, etc, eg
—'standing up for your rights'
—defending a position which you believe is correct
—simply trying to win

UNCO-OPERATIVE

Handling conflict: the options available

Usually when getting the results of any test or questionnaire, people first want to know what the right answers are. As with management style generally, there are no right answers. All five modes are useful in some situations; it depends upon that situation. The uses of each mode are described below.

However, as was discussed earlier, people tend to rely on

a prescribed range of styles, or modes, whether from learned orientations or skill. Some of the consequences of your orientations, as indicated by the questionnaire, are also included. These take the form of questions you should put to yourself.

Collaborating: assertive and co-operative

Uses

1 To find an integrative solution when both sets of concerns are too important to be compromised.
2 When your objective is to learn, eg testing your assumptions, understanding the views of others.
3 To merge insights from people with different perspectives on a problem.
4 To gain commitment by incorporating other's concerns into a consensual decision.
5 To work through hard feelings which have been interfering with an interpersonal relationship.

If you scored high:

1 Do you spend time discussing issues in depth that do not always deserve it?
2 Do you use this style as a way of diffusing responsibility for decisions, minimizing risks or postponing action?
3 Does your collaborative behaviour fail to elicit collaborative responses from others? If so, why is this?

If you scored low:

1 Is it hard for you to see differences as opportunities for joint gain or to solve problems?
2 Are subordinates uncommitted to your decisions or policies? Are their concerns being incorporated into them?

Competing: assertive and unco-operative

Uses

1 When quick decisive action is vital, eg emergencies.
2 On issues vital to organizational welfare when you know you're right.
3 To protect yourself against people who take advantage of non-competitive behaviour.

If you scored high:

1 Are you surrounded by 'yes' men? If so, is it because they have learned it's unwise to disagree with you, or have given up trying to influence you?

2 Are subordinates afraid to admit ignorance and uncertainty?

If you scored low:

1 Do you often feel powerless?
2 Do you have trouble taking a firm stand, even when you see the need?

Avoiding: unassertive and unco-operative

Uses
1 When other more important issues are pressing.
2 When you see no chance of satisfying your concerns.
3 When the potential damage of confronting a conflict outweighs the benefits of its solution.
4 To let people cool down—to reduce tensions to a productive level and to regain perspective and composure.
5 When the need for information gathering outweighs the advantages of an immediate decision.
6 When others can resolve the conflict more effectively.
7 When the issue is only symptomatic of a more basic issue.

If you scored high:

1 Does your influence and management ability suffer because people have difficulty getting your inputs on issues clearly?
2 Are important decisions made by default?

If you scored low:

1 Do you find yourself hurting people's feelings or stirring up hostilities?
2 Do you often feel hurried or overwhelmed by a number of issues?

Accommodating: unassertive and co-operative

Uses
1 When you realize that you are wrong.
2 When the issue is much more important to the other person than to you.
3 When continued competition would only damage your cause.
4 When avoiding disruption is especially important.
5 To aid in the development of subordinates—allowing them to experiment and learn from their mistakes.

If you scored high:

1 Do you feel that your own ideas and concerns are not getting the attention they deserve?

114

2 Is discipline low, and do people take advantage of it?

If you scored low:

1 Do you have trouble building goodwill with others?
2 Do others often seem to regard you as unreasonable?
3 Do you have trouble admitting it when you are wrong?

Compromising: intermediate in both assertion and co-operation

Uses

1 When goals are moderately important but not worth the effort or potential disruption of more assertive approaches.
2 Where two opponents with equal power are strongly committed to mutually exclusive goals, eg some IR bargaining.
3 To achieve temporary settlements to complex issues.
4 To arrive at expedient solutions under time pressure.
5 As a back-up when collaboration or competition fails.

If you scored high:

1 Do you concentrate so heavily upon the practicalities and tactics of compromise that you sometimes lose sight of larger issues and longer-term, strategic objectives?
2 Does an emphasis on bargaining and trading create a congenital climate of gamesmanship?

If you scored low:

1 Do you find yourself too sensitive or embarrassed to be effective in bargaining situations?
2 Do you find it hard to make concessions?

This model gives an overview, insight and understanding of conflict and its handling, and also insight into one's own orientations and practices. It can help you understand awkward conflict situations. The skill to deal with it is particularly linked with effective influencing, and those of asserting and active listening. It is also much connected with the use of positive personal power and, in some situations, the ability to cope with negative personal power.

Implicit in the approach is the ability to move the conflict from one mode to another. For example, two people may begin problem solving through collaboration, discover no integrative outcomes are successful and then settle for a compromise where the 'pie', rather than being made larger, is split. Locating a superordinate (overriding) goal is a useful way of facilitating collaboration. Equally the ability to break through a prolonged impasse, through either accommodating or competing, has merit in some situations. Generally to know what one is doing, rather than just acting from patterned behaviour, is likely to result in better outcomes as well as not leaving a legacy of bad feelings, often inner-directed.

What is of key importance is which of the three basic orientations towards outcomes is adopted. These are for win-win (Collaboration), win-lose (Competing), or lose-lose (Avoiding). A problem with win-lose outcomes is that they tend to become lose-lose ones, because often the 'losing' side makes sure that the 'winners' do not really win after all. This can happen to some extent with lose-win (Accommodating). Compromising can be seen as half win-half win.

What matters too, in transactional analysis terms, is staying in the adult ego state. This applies especially when dealing with aggression, whether it is being dumped on a person through the discharge of bad feelings or is part of a habitual response. Assertion has much to offer here, particularly some of its special techniques.

There are some special situations which require particular handling. As well as dealing with aggression, these include dealing with passive hostility and conflict between groups.

Dealing with passive hostility
Who is a passive-hostile?
Someone who won't declare their own needs or wants while at the same time judging, blaming or rejecting the other person for acting inappropriately. Usually the person is stuck between two conflicting emotions, eg anger and fear.

How do you recognize passive hostility?
—they will be giving out mixed messages
—their energy will be turned inwards rather than outwards
—they will be denying their own feelings
—they will avoid making judgements explicitly
—they will tend to be volatile
—they minimize their own needs/wants
—they often avoid taking responsibility
—they can be agitated and look disapproving
—they will be 'hard work'

Some choices in dealing with someone who is a passive-hostile
—offer feedback on mixed messages
—ask them to share their judgements
—ask them what they want
—offer judgements
—make interpretations on how they are feeling
—give them appreciation for what they're doing well

116

—express your feelings
—encourage them to do something different
—'confront' the situation

Techniques for handling aggression

There are a number of special assertion techniques that are useful when faced with aggression. Although the techniques are not primarily for this purpose, and can be used for a variety of other situations, they can be of value when one is being aggressed upon. The first of these is:

Broken record

The broken record is a useful technique to use when you want to say 'No' or otherwise set limits with someone who is having difficulty is getting your message. It is a particularly effective way of telling others what you want when their own wishes are blinding them to seeing yours. The broken record is most handy in situations where an explanation would provide the other person with an opportunity to drag out a pointless argument. It has five steps:

1 Clarify in your own mind exactly what you want or don't want.
2 Formulate a short, specific, easy to understand statement about what you want. Keep it to one sentence if you can and offer no excuses or explanation.
3 Use body language to support the statement, such as looking the other person in the eye.
4 Calmly and firmly repeat your statement as many times as necessary for the person to get your message and to realize that you won't change your mind.
5 You may choose to briefly acknowledge the other person's ideas, feelings etc before returning to your broken record but don't allow yourself to become sidetracked by the other person's statements.

Here is a dialogue that exemplifies the broken record:

CUSTOMER	SALESPERSON
'I bought this watch here a few days ago, it's not working well and I want to return it and get my money back.'	'Do you have a receipt?'

117

'Yes.'	'It says you bought the watch over a week ago. That's too long. How can you expect us to take back something you bought so long ago?'
'I understand I bought it over a week ago and I want to return it and get my money back.'	'Our store policy is that all returns must be made within one week.'
'I understand that. This watch is not working properly and I want to return it and get my money back.'	'Given the policy I wouldn't feel authorized to do that.'
'This watch isn't working properly. I want to return it and get my money back.'	'I could get into trouble for doing such a thing.'
'I hear your concern. I still want to return the watch which isn't working properly and get my money back.'	'Look, I don't want to take any chances. The manager isn't here at the moment. Why don't you return when he is.'
'This watch isn't working properly. I want to return it and get my money back, now.'	'You don't seem to appreciate the difficulty this causes me.'
'I know I may sound that way but this watch isn't working properly. I want to return it and get my money back now.'	'Okay, Okay.'

Content to process shift
This is used when the focus of a conversation is felt to be drifting away from the topic you want to talk about. You simply shift from the actual subject being discussed (the content) to the process. For example, you could say 'We have moved away from what we agreed to discuss into old history'.

Content to process shift is especially helpful when voices are being raised and both people are angry. The trick is to comment on what is going on between you in a neutral, dispassionate way so that your statements won't be experienced as an attack.

Momentary delay
You may feel under pressure to respond immediately to a situation when being pressured. If you do so you might end up doing or saying something you regret. Equally if you don't respond you may feel that you are letting others make your decisions for you.
   Momentary delays let you:

1 make sure that you understand the other person
2 analyse what has been said
3 get clear on what you think and feel about it
4 consciously influence the situation so that you are more likely to get the outcome you want

Here are some examples:

'Slow down, this is too crucial to whizz through.'
'That's interesting, let me think about that for a moment.'
'Let me make sure I understood what you were saying.'

Time out
When you know what you're discussing is important but it's at an impasse through becoming too aggressive, delay the conversation until another time.

Example:
'This is getting too heated. I want time to think about it. When's a good time for you next week to discuss it further?'

8 Non-verbal and body language: conversing without words

This chapter looks at how people converse without words and identifies significant aspects of behaviour which often take place below our level of awareness. At the end of the chapter are three suggestions for activities which add meaning to the text and which support understanding of this vital part of communication.

It has been said that we speak with our vocal organs but converse with our whole body. Every human body is constantly sending out a multitude of signals that form part of the communication we have with each other, which may explain the 'vibes' we experience about people and they about us. We communicate with our expressions, eyes, gestures and postures, our physical distance and the orientations we adopt, and the plethora of signals coming from these sources can be interpreted by the socially skilled not only to enhance the flow of social interaction but to give insights into the state of mind and feelings of the other person.

There are times when people try to hide their true feelings for reasons of politeness, expediency or whatever. Some are remarkably adept at this—politicians, used car salesmen and actors for example. For most of us though clues to our real state of mind occur through what is known as non-verbal language; that is, our body gives indications, perhaps unwittingly, as to how we feel. Often what happens is a basic conflict with what is going on inside the person in her feelings and outside her in her actions. Not unnaturally, this induces tension which is likely to show in a number of ways, as we shall explore. Such additional insight can be useful, not for any sinister or manipulative reasons, but to aid the interaction through developing a greater empathy. There are,

120

too, aspects of non-verbal behaviour which can be used to heighten considerably the effectiveness of communication whether between two people or in a group setting. It is important to stress that it is the pattern of such signals that provides the most reliable indicators and that not too much weight should be placed on isolated ones, as we can only at best make inferences from such signals.

Facial expression

The face is perhaps the area of the body that the majority of us use most consciously as a channel of non-verbal communication. Our faces are capable of transmitting complex and subtle messages when we wish and the meaning of such messages is readily evident. It is common knowledge that a face that is pleasantly smiling, alert or excited attracts strongly; one which is forlorn or helpless may stimulate others to approach and console but a tense, hard, grumpy face has the opposite effect.

Through socialization we have learned to control our expressions to a remarkable degree, and an expression may portray what its wearer wishes us to think rather than her true feelings: something at which the English are particularly adept. We talk about our 'public face', the kind worn by a hostess at a party, and our 'private face' which we wear when relaxed and alone. Although there may be some imprinting of our long-term moods in our faces which gives clues about ourselves and others—anxiety-ridden, basically happy and content or whatever—we still have a remarkable facility for controlling expressions when we choose to do so.

Thus because of the way we have learned to control our facial expressions it is sometimes difficult to detect emotional states purely from these. How often have we all smiled pleasantly while seething within? But we have less control over our eyes and eyebrows and the non-verbal communication which emanates from this part of the face can give valuable clues to the state of mind of the other person.

Eye contact

Eye contact and signals provide a particularly rich source of information about how an interaction is progressing. They are also used to control the nature and flow of the interaction. There would seem to be a smooth pattern of eye contact to which most people conform and which needs to be appropriate to maintain satisfactory interaction. Value judgements tend to be made about individuals who do not conform to the norms, for example 'shifty eyes' or a 'fixed gaze'.

When we talk we look up to get feedback on how the other person is reacting, and we tend to end long passages with a gaze that indicates that it is now the other person's turn to speak. The duration of gaze is synchronized with patterns of speech: people look nearly twice as much while listening as they do when speaking, their glances are longer and the away periods are shorter. It has been noted that we tend to look away more when delivering hesitant passages of speech, perhaps so that we can filter out some of the non-verbal signals in order to concentrate on organizing our thoughts; but with fluent, well-rehearsed parts of speech we tend to establish eye contact more. In pauses and long utterances we will look at the other person for permission to continue speaking and to obtain feedback; when we have finished we are likely to look at the other person to signal that we have finished and that she can start. Equally, it is possible to end a conversation just by not looking at the other person.

When another person looks at us, particularly in the region of the eyes, we feel he is giving us his attention. We also know that, if we accompany our conversation with the appropriate amount of eye contact, we shall be thought to be more believable, confident and favourably disposed. The conventional wisdom here has to some extent been justified as it has been established that people do look more when they like the person they are talking to. This is only one side of the picture.

Prolonged looking in the form of a direct stare or its opposite, a deliberately deflected gaze, involves intensely active feelings because of the intimacy or lack of it it engenders. A direct stare can indicate feelings of an amorous, hostile or fearful kind; a deflected gaze shyness, casual superiority or downcast submissiveness. Because there are only two kinds of gazing, towards and away, we have to take note of other body signals to infer which of the three basic moods are involved. Prolonged looking combined with a friendly expression conveys a wish to be friendly, or sexual attraction; but combined with a hostile expression or other clues it means that one person dislikes another or wishes to dominate him. Depending on the relationship the other person wishes to establish he or she will look back in an appropriate way: deflecting his or her gaze, for example, if the response is one of submissiveness to the other person's hostility and dominance.

Both passive dominance and passive submissiveness involve exaggerated looking away. Passive submissiveness is perhaps a response well-known to some schoolteachers; passive dominance is where a person is so casual and contemptuous about his dominance over another person—the boss gazing out of the window while reprimanding a subordinate for example—that he makes himself remote from him by not displaying any intimacy through eye contact. It is the clearest possible indication of the worthlessness of the other person.

The degree of dilation of the pupils has also been found to give accurate indications of the state of mind of the other person and, unlike facial expressions, these are almost impossible to control. The difficulty here is that in practical terms one has to look so intensely to detect changes that this act in itself impedes rather than helps interaction.

Physical proximity and territorial behaviour

Each of us has as it were our own personal space or portable territory which is carried around with us and which we intuitively adjust according to the desired intimacy of the situation. There are large cultural differences about what is an appropriate distance between people; for example, English people generally keep a greater physical distance between themselves and others than Arabs or Latin Americans, so that what may seem comfortable to an Arab may seem uncomfortably close to an Englishman. At many a cocktail party an Englishman may be seen politely walking backwards, glass in hand and conversation flowing, closely pursued by an Arab.

At many a cocktail party an Englishman may be seen politely walking backwards

We thus tend to guard our personal space and adjust our reactions to the social situation as we define it or when space is limited. If a number of people are crushed together in a lift or tube train so that they have no choice about their personal space being violated, a way of coping with this is to define the other people as non-persons so that the normal implications of physical proximity to others no longer applies. Equally, if there is just one person sitting in a waiting-room and another person who enters chooses to sit next to him, the implications here are different from the more usual case—where there is choice of maintaining some distance.

Physical proximity is therefore another important aspect of non-verbal communication, particularly in relation to intimacy (both non-sexual and sexual) and dominance, and the distances at which

123

people interact correspond with the type of encounter. In Britain this is, typically, for intimate friends 0–18 inches, casual friends 30 to 48 inches, and for social consultative situations 4 to 12 feet (figure 29). In fact, by observing two people from a distance, one can guess with a reasonable degree of accuracy the relationship between them from how physically close, or separate, they are. It is no accident that the saying 'keeping someone at arm's length' has become part of our language.

Figure 29
Interaction zones

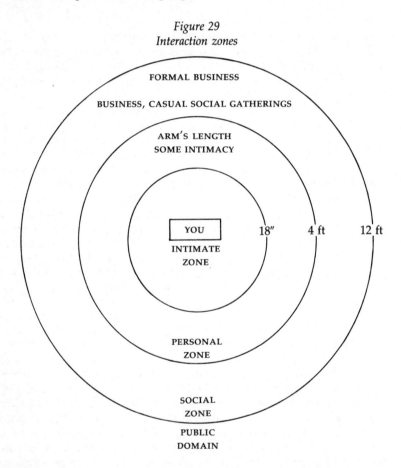

Thus in an interview it matters how close the interviewer sits to the interviewee if he wants the conversation to be relaxed and open. Too close is likely to cause the interviewee to feel threatened or embarrassed, too far away can induce the formal atmosphere beloved by selection boards. There are, too, a number of other factors which include the relative status of the parties, physical territory (which is part of the psychological territory) and the orientations or positions that the people take up to each other.

Status confers with it the right to more personal space, as observation of many of the more senior managers of an organization will confirm. Often a big desk protects such an enlarged social zone by providing a barrier from those whose worth does not warrant inclusion in the ambience. Of course, for the other person to sit on the desk, if he dares, displays a one-up-manship to exceed that of the person whose territory it is, and is likely to result in a change of position if that person attempts to regain his status advantage. Alternatively, in an interview, where the interviewer does not want to use his status over the interviewee but wants a less formal conversation he will use the rules of space accordingly.

It also matters in whose physical territory the encounter takes place. Although the case that man is a territorial animal, in the way that many other species are, has been somewhat overstated the majority of us do feel more comfortable and relaxed when 'on our own ground'. Those familiar with open plan office layouts will have observed how people will find ways of staking out their own personal territories. There are elaborate rules to govern the way we behave when in our own or entering someone else's territory. In social encounters we tend to act when in someone else's home in a way that reflects the territorial prerogatives of that person; in our own home we feel the obligation of the host and are likely to feel more relaxed and secure. To a large extent these rules are carried over into work so that it matters where an interaction takes place. As an example of this it may be more profitable for the boss to carry out some interviews in the subordinate's office and to visit rather than summon him when she wants to discuss a problem in a low key way. Equally the territorial prerogative can be used to the opposite effect.

The orientations or physical positions relative to other persons that people take up can also have important effects and conse-quences. If a person is sitting along the longer side of a rectangular table and another person joins him, he has the choice of sitting beside him, opposite him or at right angles to him. If he defines the situation as one of cooperation he will usually sit alongside the other person; if he wants to compete, negotiate or sell something he will sit opposite him; if he wishes to hold a discussion or conversation he usually chooses to sit at right angles. Thus people take up a body orientation with others according to how they define that situation. This may have something to do with the volume of non-verbal signals they perceive to be appropriate, so that the greater the intimacy of the situation the more the non-verbal signals are dispensed with. When the seating arrangements are obligatory there is a tendency for people who sit opposite each other to compete and for those who sit alongside each other to cooperate. As any experienced committee man knows, who sits where can have a crucial effect on the outcome of a meeting and it is fascinating to see the way in which places are taken around a meeting table according to the roles that people wish to play (*see* chapter 10, Meetings: face to face with a group).

Thus the rules of physical proximity, status, territory and orientations are ones that can be used to good effect to influence the 'music' of any interaction. The interviewer who wishes to carry out a probing selection interview requiring non-defensive responses is likely to sit at right angles to the interviewee and within her social encounter zone, in a territory which is as neutral as possible (perhaps away from his desk), and to dispense with many of his status differential devices.

Body contact

Physical proximity has an obvious connection with body contact, which is one of the most primitive forms of communication. Again there are great cross cultural differences between socially acceptable norms of body contact and this form of social communication is less common in Britain than most other countries. Certain forms of touching—shaking hands, back patting—are socially acceptable forms of intimacy while others are taboo, probably because of possible sexual connotations. In other cultures, such as the US, Arab and African countries, a greater degree of body contact is preferred, and British visitors to these countries may be disconcerted by the amount of back slapping and arm touching they encounter. The Briton in contrast may appear to others as distant and aloof, with obvious implications for the relationship.

Gestures and body postures

We have all attended meetings where the amount of shuffling of posteriors and rustling of papers has indicated clearly that the meeting has gone on too long. Many other gestures and postures, although less obvious than this, can give valuable insights to the other person's inner mood. Some of these are displacement movements, the kind of agitated actions we display during periods of inner tension and nervousness. These can be readily seen at airport departure lounges or in doctors' and interview waiting rooms. Fiddling with a watch strap, continual tapping of a cigarette to remove ash and polishing of spectacle lenses are examples of our need to find, albeit unconsciously, an action to perform to relieve some stress we may be experiencing. Most of us use

126

displacement activities at various times so that we often develop our own personal displacement habits. Common ones are some of the activities which go with smoking, ritual hand washing, displacement grooming, such as smoothing down clothes that are already smooth, tidying or the displacement nibbling and drinking that often occurs particularly at parties. Displacement activities are indicators of how at ease a person is in a particular situation.

On the other hand intention movements, which are small preparatory movements, give clues about what we intend to do. Sometimes they are not carried through into the full movement of behaviour; instead we hesitate and only carry out the first or intention part of the movement. There is then a double clue: we want to do something but are hesitant to do so. A classic case of this is in indicating that we want an interaction to cease by carrying out the first part of the movement of rising from a chair or, if standing, posturing our body so that we are about to move away. We want to leave but something, politeness perhaps, prevents us from doing so. At a meeting, intention movements can be seen when someone wants to make a contribution but perhaps can't find the opportunity or nerve to do so.

As well as these there are other sets of gestures and postures which form part of the repertoire of non-verbal communication. While some are intended to communicate a definite message, such as a lecturer describing a shape with her hands as well as her voice, others are not. Although more difficult to interpret, these again provide useful clues to the inner mood of the other person. Care is needed not to infer too much from a single action; a person may scratch his leg simply to relieve an itch and not from any deeper motive. Rather, if the movements form a pattern with other clues, we shall be on much surer ground in inferring the emotional state of the other person.

Many gestures have their roots in childhood or instinct. Certainly many of them are very common. Mothers, for instance, whether left or right handed, hold their babies with the baby's ear to the mother's heart, and it is established that the most effective rocking to comfort babies is that of a frequency that corresponds with heart beats. A good many gestures are concerned with self-touching. Touching our own body is a form of self intimacy through contact with ourselves which provides comfort. Holding hands with ourselves is an example of this, which has its roots in the physical comfort we derived from our parents when children. Often forms of self-touching of the face, mouth or supporting one's jaw when it doesn't need support can indicate mild stress. The person who has his arms tightly crossed across his body is in an unconscious embrace with himself, and is likely to be feeling threatened, particularly if his legs are also crossed. It is as though he is forming

127

a protective barrier about himself. Hands held on the back of the neck is another classic defensive gesture. The person who is feeling non-threatened and relaxed will typically take up a relaxed, non-self embracing posture. When a person is emotionally aroused his gestures and movements tend to be more diffuse and apparently pointless. Legs and feet are of special interest as they are less controlled than other areas of the body and provide particular giveaways when not screened by a desk.

One example of a posture which indicates some wish to dominate, and one not infrequently used by schoolmasters, is standing straight with the chin held up. But leaning forward and smiling indicates warmth and encouragement. As a general rule we use head movements, by giving nods, to indicate that we are listening to the other person and giving him encouragement to go on.

The position of the hands can give some useful clues about levels of assertiveness. Generally, the higher the level at which the hands are positioned the more assertive is that person. Typical hand position gestures reducing down the assertiveness scale are the grasping of lapels, thumbs in waistcoat, hands in jacket side pockets (much beloved by royalty, admirals and political leaders) and hands in trouser pockets. This latter is so relaxed and unassertive that in some situations, particularly authoritarian ones, it is regarded as inappropriate. An interesting exception to the hand level/assertiveness general rule is the thumbs in belt position which, although fairly low down the body, is an assertiveness giveaway.

The total set of body language that goes to make up a posture can be particularly revealing in reflecting attitudes to the other people in the interaction, eg inattention, emotion, or the formal and informal status afforded the other person. When silent films were taken of managers entering the offices of other managers it was quite clear to people who were shown these films which manager was the senior and how friendly they were. It is perhaps a sobering thought that the regard, or lack of it, that we have for others is displayed so clearly.

It is also possible to deduce something of the past background of an individual from his bearing, an old soldier for example, and the way such behaviour is carried over into a new situation tells us something about the image the person has of himself.

Postural echo

Next time you see people talking informally, whom you know are friends, you may notice that they may be adopting similar body postures. Here they are not deliberately imitating one another, rather it is one form of a 'postural echo' display of companionship.

When they talk movements are synchronized between them. It is as if acting in unison cements the bond they share. If in a group such as a social gathering one person is different in posture from the others it destroys the 'ease' of the group causing the others to take appropriate action to restore their harmony by soothing, paying attention to, rejecting that person or whatever.

When an interviewer sees an interviewee taking up a posture that reflects his own it provides an indication to him that their relationship has reached a stage where the other person is relatively at ease. Equally the interviewer may take up a postural echo reflecting the other person to induce this type of relationship. One variation is for a subordinate to unnerve someone of higher status than himself by deliberately copying his actions.

In a meeting it is possible to see sub-groups taking up particular postural echoes to indicate which one its members align to and to indicate their difference from other ones. It is sometimes possible to see someone changing sides by his change in posture before he verbally declares his intention to do so. Chairmen often take up an intermediate 'I'm neutral' posture.

Paralinguistics

The chapter started with the verbal content of communication being carefully distinguished from the non-verbal aspects. However, it would be incomplete not to comment on some of the paralinguistic aspects, that is non-verbal elements of speech, such as an encouraging grunt or the emotional tone of voice. It is possible, for example, to read emotional states not only by what is said but the way in which it is said. Loudness, pitch and speed are all important. An aggressive person talks loudly, an anxious person faster than normal and at a higher pitch, a depressed person more slowly and quietly. Some habits like the over use of particular mannerisms or 'ums' and 'ers' can irritate others to distraction. Many of us have speech habits that we have been unaware of until listening to ourselves on a tape recorder.

Summary

Non-verbal aspects of communication, as well as being a fascinating subject in its own right, can provide valuable clues about how an interaction is progressing and the state of mind of the other person. An understanding of the rules involved can also aid the conduct of the interaction, particularly as far as the 'music' is concerned.

A number of provisos must be stressed. The meanings of body signals are inferred and subject to misinterpretation. A greater reliability can be placed on them when they form a pattern and are considered with other clues. It also matters whether the intent of the person using the insights is honest or manipulative. If it is the latter, it will in any event show and influence the 'music'. People may not be able to explain why; they will simply feel the 'vibes' ironically picked up in an intuitive way from the 'non verbal leakage' of the other person.

Activity plans: non-verbal and body language

The text has described the significance of non-verbal behaviour and body language. The activity plans suggest ways in which you can explore this fascinating aspect of relationships, much of which usually takes place below our level of awareness.

Activity 1: casual observation: non-verbal and body language

You have an enormous choice of subjects for casual observation. Observe individuals and groups in different social settings, if possible without listening to the words. Public transport, pubs or restaurants, parties and family groups will give a good variety of social contexts. If you have qualms about this kind of 'man-watching', observe situations on television instead. For example, it can be an interesting exercise to observe a TV play with the sound off, occasionally switching on to check your interpretations. Look for the factors listed below and consider their meaning in terms of relationships and feelings:

   facial expression
   eye contact
   physical proximity and territorial behaviour
   body contact
   gestures and body postures
   paralinguistics.

Activity 2: observation by agreement with feedback

If it is possible to do, a fruitful means of developing awareness in these areas is to observe, interpret and then check your conclusions with those observed. Similarly, others who are interested may agree to give you feedback on your own non-verbal behaviour.

This activity can be carried out by an agreement with those involved in a number of ways. You can exchange views upon your 'here and now' non-verbal behaviour. Another possibility is to describe yourselves as you have observed each other in the past. A third option is to agree to interject feedback during future interactions.

130

Activity 3: self observation
Listen to your own body language. It may have messages for you.

9 Interviewing: face to face with another

The first section of this chapter defines the interview, describes different styles, identifies characteristics of good and bad interviewers and makes points for guidance.

The second section, the activity plan, is developed from the text. This suggests things that the reader may wish to do in order to develop skills and knowledge about interviewing or any face to face contact.

What is an interview?
Interviewing is a key skill for managers and supervisors. It has been shown that a substantial part of their time at work can be spent interacting with another person. In this sense, an interview is simply a conversation between two people with an organizational purpose. It is not just for recruitment, although this usually springs most readily to mind. The interview may be for staff development, appraisal, discipline, counselling, negotiation, briefing, information seeking and so on. Sometimes interviews are formal and sometimes they are so informal that it is not clear who is interviewing whom.

So the type of interview varies and differing approaches are required. One way of describing these differences is in terms of styles of interviewing.

Styles of interviewing
The interviewer's style or pattern of behaviour towards the interviewee can vary in the degree of directiveness shown. Directiveness can be assessed by the latitude allowed to the interviewee to take the initiative during the interview. It is also characterized by the

kind of questions which the interviewer asks and the extent to which the interviewee is made to feel the junior partner. The two extremes can be described as directive and non-directive. The middle position can be called 'patterned', or a planned conversation.

No single style is appropriate to all interviews; in certain kinds of interview the directive style is appropriate, in others the non-directive. The trick is to recognize the different styles and to choose the approach which is appropriate to the interviewee and the interview purpose. Sometimes, however, interviewers tend to use their status unconsciously and are directive when less directive styles would be more successful.

Figure 30
Styles of interviewing

	DIRECTIVE	PATTERNED	NON-DIRECTIVE
interviewer's role	interrogator	conversation guide	counsellor
relations with interviewee	boss-subordinate	equals	helper
latitude given to interviewee to influence the interview	very little	some	a great deal
plan/agenda	rigid adherence	flexible	free
flow	interviewer sets the pace and interrupts the interviewee	interviewer supports and steers the interviewee's flow	interviewer supports flow, builds upon replies and waits out pauses
sharing the talking	a great deal, perhaps most, from the interviewer	evenly shared, with perhaps most from the interviewee	most from the interviewee
types of question	a high proportion of 'closed' and 'leading' questions	a high proportion of 'open-ended' with some 'reflecting back' questions	a high proportion of 'reflecting back' with some 'open-ended' questions

The directive style certainly takes less time. It is appropriate where factual information is being sought and the interviewer knows exactly what is wanted and the interviewee is willing to give it.

133

The problems may be that the interviewee could be put on the defensive because of insufficient freedom of expression and also the relationship between the two individuals may be impaired.

The non-directive style consumes more time, but is appropriate for exploring sensitive matters and understanding feelings and attitudes. It is the style for the counselling interview.

The patterned style is appropriate for interviews which are seen by the interviewer as planned conversations in the context of an adult to adult relationship and an organizational purpose. Senior recruitment, promotion and appraisal interviews may fall into this category.

It is largely the types of questions asked that characterize the style used. There are six basic types of questioning patterns (*see* figure 31 opposite).

A directive style is more likely to have a higher proportion of types 1 and 2; a patterned style 3, 4 and 5; and a non-directive style 5 and 6.

Characteristics of good and bad interviewers

Irrespective of style and question types, there are certain interviewer characteristics which help or hinder an interview from the interviewee's viewpoint. The features which were mentioned most frequently in a study conducted by Robin Evenden are indicated in figure 32 on page 136. All interviewers will have a mixture of good and bad points, some of which may be deeply ingrained. Many of the features can be developed or curtailed through awareness and practice. The activity plan at the end of the chapter is designed to help you do this in an interesting way.

Words and music: facts and feeling: task and process

In figure 32, the category A characteristics are to do with the procedure of the interview and the exchange of facts or opinions. This aspect of the interview is sometimes referred to as the TASK activity because it is concerned with regulating the exchange of WORDS necessary to achieve the interview purpose, or task in hand. Any confusion or lack of clarity here is identified by the interviewee as hindering the interview. However, it is not the only factor seen as contributing to success or failure. Category C characteristics refer to things like being relaxed or tense, showing understanding or indifference, and humour or coldness. These are part of the other inevitable ingredient of a face to face contact or interview. They are about the relationship between the two people and the feelings generated. It is often referred to as the interaction PROCESS, or the MUSIC of the interview.

134

Figure 31
Styles of interviewing: different types of questions

STYLES OF INTERVIEWING	DIFFERENT TYPES OF QUESTION	EXAMPLES
DIRECTIVE ↑ PATTERNED ↓ NON-DIRECTIVE	1 *Closed questions* Questions which produce only short answers, like 'yes' or 'no'	eg Do you play golf?
	2 *Leading questions* Questions which lead the interviewee to give the answer the interviewer hopes to hear	eg Golf is my favourite sport. Of course, you do play, don't you?
	3 *Controlling questions* Questions which help the interviewer control the interview	eg Thanks for telling me about your sporting interests. Would you tell me about your work experience?
	4 *Probing or building questions* Questions which build upon an answer already given; which extend enquiry into a particular subject	eg Why did you say you like people who play golf?
	5 *Open-ended questions* Questions which give opportunity for a lengthy answer	eg What are your leisure interests?
	6 *Reflecting back questions* Questions which restate a reply; which test the interviewer's understanding	eg So you play golf every week then?

Some aspects of the interview can affect both the task and process, or words and music, at the same time. The items mentioned by the interviewees in category B seem to do this. For example, if the interviewer talks too much it could produce bad feelings in the interviewee, while at the same time reducing the flow of words which may be necessary to achieve the task purpose.

The climate of the interview
The climate of the interview is affected by the behaviour of the individuals involved and in turn it influences the task activity. It

135

Figure 32
Interviewers: characteristics helping and hindering the interview

HELPING		HINDERING
A TASK (WORDS; PROCEDURAL)		
Well prepared and briefed		Unprepared
Makes purpose and method clear		No clarity of purpose or method
Systematic		Disjointed
Clear questions/ statements		Unclear questions/statements
B MIXED		
Allows interviewee to complete answer		Interrupts
Attentive/listens		Inattentive/doesn't listen
Encourages interviewee to talk		Talks too much
Clear voice		Irritating characteristics of speech/manner
C PROCESS (MUSIC)		
Relaxed		Tense
Puts interviewee at ease		Creates tension in interviewee
Understands interviewee's viewpoint/fears		Indifference to interviewee's viewpoint/fears
Respects interviewee's self esteem		Undermines interviewee's confidence
Shows sense of humour		Distant and impersonal

Hindering: the interviewer talks too much

is therefore vital that the interviewer should be aware of the need to establish rapport and to reduce any tension in the situation. This means learning to read the music of interaction and to monitor the impact of one's own behaviour. How can this be achieved? (*see* figure 33 overleaf).

Playing a prisoner in the film *Cool Hand Luke*, Paul Newman described a confused and sadistic warder as not knowing whether to 'spit, smile or swallow'. This neatly describes the whole range of possible emotional reactions to another person or event. The behaviour which produces these responses is called 'social emotional'. Social because it affects a relationship; emotional because it influences feelings. These are the notes of the human music process and the good interviewer will usually try to behave in a social emotional positive way, in order to produce a 'smile' reaction from the interviewee.

The good interviewer will usually try to behave in a social emotional positive way in order to produce a 'smile' reaction from the interviewee

Interviewing: practical points for guidance

As each interview is to some degree uniquely different there can be no set way or 'magic formula' for conducting them effectively, but there are some general practical points it is useful to consider. In doing so it is important that the interviewer concentrates not only upon the words exchanged but also the music created, because this significantly affects the outcome and future relationships. He can monitor his impact by keeping in mind such considerations as:

What am I trying to achieve?
What respect for the interviewee am I showing?
Am I *really* listening to the other person?
Is my style appropriate?

137

Figure 33
Interaction process analysis: listen to the music you make

TYPE OF BEHAVIOUR	EXAMPLES	IMPACT ON OTHER'S FEELINGS/ RELATIONSHIP	IMPACT ON TASK ACHIEVEMENT
SOCIAL EMOTIONAL POSITIVE	1 *indicating acceptance and warmth* such as shaking hands, welcoming, giving encouragement, showing admiration and accepting offers of help 2 *releasing tension*, such as making jokes 3 *agreement*, including non-verbal acts which show interest, such as head nodding	smile	supports the word flow needed to achieve task objective
TASK — TELLS / ASKS	Facts, opinions, suggestions	neutral	words needed to achieve the task (appraisal selection/ discipline)
SOCIAL EMOTIONAL NEGATIVE	1 *indicating unfriendliness*, such as ridicule, teasing, threatening, impudence, or interrupting 2 *creating tension*, by displaying anxiety 3 *disagreement with* the content of what has been said, although the effect of this can be reduced by the manner of disagreement	spit (anger) or swallow (withdraw)	music of anger drowns the words or the other person goes into a shell and words cease

Am I asking the right type of question?
Am I testing my pre-interview assumptions?
What is my spit, smile or swallow impact?
Am I talking too much?
Is my 'steering' adequate?

Before the interview

Decide the objective
What do I want to achieve as an outcome of the interview? This is an important and often neglected question. For example, do I want to chastise a subordinate for causing an accident or to change his attitude to safety? Do I need to retain his goodwill? Questions like

this need to be considered so that the interview will be conducted in an appropriate way.

The objective will also give a yardstick against which the outcome of the interview can be assessed.

Prepare

What facts do I need? What facts should the interviewee have? What approach should I adopt? What are the key areas we should cover? It is certainly worth investing time in considering these questions before any significant interview. It is also necessary to avoid sticking rigidly to a plan should circumstances overtake it, as they often do in the dynamics of human relationships. Preparation should not limit the interviewer's flexibility during the interview. It is not always possible to spend time in preparation—some interviews occur spontaneously and others will not wait for preparation. If someone is in a high state of agitation or anxiety it may be more productive to carry out the interview right away, rather than to postpone it in order to prepare.

Choose time and place

At what time of day will it be held and how long will it take? Where should the interview take place and what room arrangements are needed? There are many points that can be taken into account when answering these questions.

For example, the result would probably be better if the interviewee had the chance to quietly reflect upon the interview outcome; the end of the working day would be the best time. Or perhaps anxiety would grow through the day, which could mean it would be better to conduct the interview earlier. Some interviews might benefit from the formality of the interviewer's office, others on his home ground and even others in a local pub.

The room setting can greatly affect the music or relationship during the interview. Keeping the interviewee waiting, placing a desk between you, seating him on a low chair at a distance, and making sure that the sun is in his eyes whilst you drink your tea when he remains thirsty are ways of creating an interview climate. Punctuality, chairs of the same height placed at right angles, no desk as a barrier, comfort, privacy and courtesy are other ways of influencing the atmosphere.

How the interview is arranged also requires some thought. If someone is summoned without warning, particularly if he or she does not know why and is otherwise engaged at the time, he is hardly likely to arrive in a non-defensive relaxed frame of mind. As a general rule it is better to set up the interview in advance, ideally at a time reasonably convenient to both parties. For some interviews, particularly those where timing is not critical, it may be better to choose an occasion which follows on naturally from some other event. Thus a manager may choose to initiate a counselling interview to follow on from a regular meeting she has with a member of her staff. Where circumstances permit, there is merit in awaiting the right moment. There are thus many choices to be made before the interview which may have a substantial impact upon its success.

During the interview
Put at their ease
One of the prime tasks of the interviewer is to establish an atmosphere which supports the exchange of information. The early stage is important for setting the tone.

The way to put a person at ease will depend upon that person and the situation. If you have ever interviewed school leavers for their first job you may have found that with some you had to talk about all kinds of general things: football, the journey to the plant or whatever, before the interviewee has been sufficiently at ease to talk coherently about himself. Equally when two people have known each other for some time delay in coming to the point can induce unease on the part of the interviewee.

Establish procedure
It is also vital to establish or clarify expectations about what will be happening during the interview. The interviewee needs to learn the ground rules and what will be expected from him.

Control and the use of appropriate questions
The prime skill in interviewing is for the interviewer to guide the discussion along the path it needs to follow for the objective to be achieved. This is what is meant by control, not monopolizing the 'air time' or continually interrupting the interviewee. Control is largely exercised by the appropriate use of questions. One advantage of open-ended questions is that they tend to produce a richer source of information, including indications of feelings and attitudes. The discussion is also likely to flow more naturally if this approach is taken, as the next question tends to arise spontaneously from the previous answer, eg:

What is it that you hope to find in this job?
I think the opportunity to do more responsible and challenging work
What kind of things do you have in mind?
To have more say in what I do and how I do it
And how does that work out in your present job?

Not very well, I am one of a group and my boss runs things
   pretty tightly

How do you feel your boss should manage then?

By leaving me alone to get on with it, after all I know a lot more
   about the job than he does

And what about working as a member of a group, what are your
   feelings about that?

It is better if everyone just gets on with his bit, it's much more
   efficient this way and there are no distractions.

Here useful insights have been obtained about the interviewee's
attitudes to fellow-workers and the kind of management style he
prefers by asking open-ended questions which build on the replies
to the previous ones. This is good control by the interviewer by
steering the conversation in such a way that the information he
requires flows naturally from it. Despite the advantages that open-
ended questions offer there are occasions when other questioning
patterns are more appropriate. In fact skilled interviewers rarely
keep to one mode of questioning throughout.

This can be illustrated by reversing the roles, so to speak. Think
about a selection interview where you are the candidate. If you
are asked open-ended questions, this is probably to your advantage
as it allows you the opportunity to provide much relevant information about yourself. Should you find the questioning pattern
changing to a patterned or closed form, you can take this as an
indication that you have been responding in a too rambling, non-
relevant way and should modify your answers accordingly.

Controlling, guiding the conversation along the path it needs to
follow, is largely achieved by the use of appropriate questions.

Listen

It is a matter of common courtesy to listen attentively and not to
allow oneself to be distracted. Over and above this, listening is
another key skill for interviewers. Much useful information can be
gleaned not only from what is said but what is not said, inflections,
nuances, strength of feeling, pauses, hesitations etc. A hesitation
before replying 'Yes' may mean that the interviewee is not really
sure. A greater inflection in the voice of someone who is relatively
unemotional may mean that he feels particularly strongly about a
certain matter; a raised voice from someone who normally talks
loudly may, have a lesser significance.

One problem people new to interviewing often encounter is that
they are so busy formulating the next question or reassuring
themselves by looking at papers that they do not really listen to
the interviewee and miss much useful information. The use
of open-ended questions, from which replies further questions

develop spontaneously, is one way of coping with this problem.

Avoid emotive and jargon language
Many people are sensitive about certain topics: age, competence, skill and appearance are common examples. When such subjects need to be discussed, the use of emotive phrases which trigger off strong adverse reaction are usually best avoided. Phrases like 'You're getting past it', 'Your dress isn't decent', 'You need some intelligence to do that job', are not exactly guaranteed to allow a particular problem to be discussed in a productive way. Jargon can also cause difficulties. Not only is there the problem of the other person not understanding, and perhaps being unwilling to show it, but jargon can create a number of other barriers. When feeling defensive, some managers have a tendency to resort to depersonalized officialese:

> the company, with due regard for procedure and precedent, has considered this matter comprehensively and has concluded that, in line with previous practice, the departures suggested, while undoubtedly not without merit, can best be reconsidered in the fulness of time and as the situation develops.

'Officialese gobbledegook' rarely creates the right kind of 'music.'

Restatements and pauses
Some interviewers find pauses embarrassing or uncomfortable, and tend to fill the pause by continuing to talk. There are advantages in 'sitting out' pauses as they often enable a person to say things that are hard to say or to clear his thoughts. Reflecting back by restating is also a useful technique which has a number of benefits. For example, it indicates that the interviewer has been listening and is interested, and can help the interviewee to clear his mind or see his problem or point of view in perspective.

Don't make judgements too early
A pitfall to avoid is making judgements too early before you have obtained sufficient information. As well as the more obvious danger of stereotyping, eg 'people who have red hair lose their temper easily', there may be more subtle influences at work. The so called halo effect means that we tend to relate more and be more favourably disposed towards those within our own halo, that is, people of the same background, interests etc as ourselves. It is also natural perhaps that we should like some people more than others. The difficulty may be in separating out the facts from our feelings about an individual: because we like one person it is easy to be favourably disposed to what he has to say and less favourably disposed to the viewpoint of someone else.
142

Conclude and summarize

There comes a natural time in any interview when the useful discussion is done and the task of the interviewer is to conclude it in an effective way. With practice this natural point is readily recognizable. At the conclusion of the interview it may often pay to summarize what has been agreed, otherwise misunderstandings may occur. The next stage in the process should also be outlined and future action indicated.

Post interview

Notes

It is better to write down thoughts while they are fresh in the mind. There is no general rule for taking notes during the interview, except that if notes be taken they should be brief and not distract from the interview itself. In some situations the taking of brief notes does indicate to the interviewee that what he is saying is being regarded as sufficiently important for notes to be taken about it. In other types of interview, perhaps of a sensitive nature, note taking can have an inhibiting effect.

Action and follow up

Quite simply, the interviewer should carry out any action which he agreed to initiate and follow up the future action agreed with the other person.

Self appraise

Every interview provides a learning experience and opportunity to develop skills. The trick is to spend two or three minutes immediately after to evaluate one's performance, using the kind of frameworks that have been discussed. If this is done and the outcome compared with the objectives set, interviewing skills can be much developed. Other ways of enhancing skills are given in the activity plans which follow.

Activity plans

The plans suggest activities designed to bring to life the text on interviewing in a way which will develop your skill and knowledge. Some suggestions will require tape or cassette recorders; others will need the willing assistance of another person or a small group. With a little ingenuity and creativity you will have an enjoyable and productive learning experience which you will be able to use to real advantage.

143

Activity 1: interviewing, style and skill assessment
You will need an interview to assess and learn from.

Suggestions:
1. recall a recent interview in which you have been involved
2. observe an interview on television
3. take part in a mock interview with a friend. Make it spontane-ous. Both parties should be themselves and not character act.

Possible subjects:
a newspaper reporter interviewing a member of the public upon a controversial topic
a recruitment interview
a two person problem situation, with which you are both familiar
a normal conversation which has some purpose, eg planning a holiday

You will find it helpful if you can record the interview.

Use all or some of the following frameworks as a means of assessing the interview and the two people taking part. The interviewer may complete a self-assessment and also be assessed by the interviewee.

Other people may be helpful as observers, using the frameworks, and discussing their observations with you.

Interview observation framework 1

Interviewer style assessment (see also figure 30)
Where do you feel the interviewer was most often during the interview on the following scales?

What part did the interviewer play?

1	2	3	4	5	6
interrogator		conversation guide		counsellor	

What was the interviewer's relationship with the interviewee?

1	2	3	4	5	6
boss-subordinate		equals		helper-helped	

How much freedom did the interviewer allow the interviewee to influence proceedings?

```
    1           2           3           4           5           6
    |_____|_____|_____|_____|_____|
  very little                    some                  a great deal
```

Was the interviewer's agenda or plan?

```
    1           2           3           4           5           6
    |_____|_____|_____|_____|_____|
   rigid                       flexible                    free
```

How was the amount of talking shared?

```
    1           2           3           4           5           6
    |_____|_____|_____|_____|_____|
  mostly the                   half and                mostly the
  interviewer                    half                  interviewee
```

Add the score on each of the scales.

  5–10 shows that a directive style was used.
  11–20 shows that a patterned or planned conversation style was used.
  21–30 shows that a non-directive style was used.

Which style would have been most appropriate for the interview?

Interview observation framework 2

Interviewer questioning technique profile (see also figure 31)
Indicate in which categories the interviewer's questions fell. If you
are listening to the interview, place a tick in the appropriate box
whenever a particular kind of question is asked.

A directive questioning technique would have a higher proportion in 1 and 2; a patterned technique most in 3, 4 and 5; and a
non-directive technique in 5 and 6. What do you think of the
profile which emerged?

TYPE OF QUESTION	FREQUENCY
1 *Closed questions* Questions producing only short answers, like 'Yes' or 'No'	
2 *Leading questions* Questions which lead the interviewee to give the answer the interviewer hopes to hear	
3 *Controlling questions* Questions which change the direction of the conversation and introduce a new subject	
4 *Probing or building questions* Questions which build upon an answer already given; which extend enquiry into a particular subject	
5 *Open-ended questions* Questions which give opportunity for a lengthy answer	
6 *Reflecting back questions* Questions that restate a reply; test the interviewer's understanding	

Interview observation framework 3

Interviewing: good and bad characteristics (see also **figure** 32)
Where do you feel the interviewer was most often during the
interview on the following scales? Add your own items if you
wish.

HELPING THE INTERVIEW		HINDERING THE INTERVIEW
	1 2 3 ¦ 4 5 6	
well prepared		unprepared
makes purpose and method clear		no clarity of purpose or method
systematic		disjointed
clear questions/ statements		unclear questions/ statements
allows interviewee to complete answer		interrupts
attentive/ listens		inattentive/ does not listen
encourages interviewee to talk		talks too much
clear voice/ pleasant manner		irritating characteristics of speech/manner
relaxed		tense
puts interviewee at ease		creates tension in interviewee
appears to understand interviewee's views/fears		indifference to interviewee's views/fears
respects interviewee's self esteem		undermines interviewee's confidence
shows sense of humour		distant and impersonal
your own items		

Average the scores on the scales to get a rating of the interviewer characteristics—1–2 suggests excellent characteristics
2–3 suggests very good characteristics
3–4 suggests average characteristics
4–5 suggests some room for improvement
5–6 suggests that the interviewer needs to work at the problems

Category of comment/act	Interviewer		Interviewee	
	Scores and examples	Total	Scores and examples	Total
SOCIAL EMOTIONAL POSITIVE Anything which produces good feelings in the other person, or helps the relationship. Showing warmth, encouragement, jokes, agreement, including non-verbal things such as tone and gesture				
TASK Facts, opinions, suggestions. No impact on feelings TELLS / ASKS				
SOCIAL EMOTIONAL NEGATIVE Anything which produces bad feelings in the other person, or hinders the relationship, whether intended or not. Ridicule, threats, interrupting, disagreeing and anything putting down the other person, including non-verbal acts.				

Interview observation framework 4

Interaction process analysis: listening to the music you make (see also figure 33)

Score each comment/action by placing a tick in the appropriate box every time something is said or done. A speech may consist of several comments before the other person talks again. These comments may fall into more than one category. If you can, briefly note examples of social emotional behaviour.

This framework can be used to analyse a recording of your interview; or to score an interview you are observing; or as a basis for discussion.

Some discussion points:

1 What effect did the social emotional comments have on the interviewee and the interviewer?
2 What do the scores tell you about 'sharing' the talking?
3 What do you think about the proportions of social emotional and task behaviour?

Activity 2: listening, how attentive are you?

The 'talking stick'

Most people are inattentive and poor listeners. They 'hear' many things, most often from inside themselves, rather than the words actually spoken by another person.

Listening is obviously a key interpersonal and interview skill. The 'talking stick' exercise is designed as an amusing and interesting way to develop the skills and experience the problems of being attentive, actually listening and not interrupting.

The exercise

1 Get a small group together to talk about any interesting topic
2 Have a 'talking stick' which can be any object
3 Only the person holding the 'stick' is allowed to speak
4 That person chooses when to pass the 'stick', at random, to another member of the group
5 The person receiving the 'stick' must repeat the last eight words spoken by the giver (or 10 or 12, depending how difficult you wish to make it), and then continue the conversation
6 The conversation ends at an agreed time.

If you want an 'attentiveness rating' an observer can record the number of words each individual remembered each time the 'stick' was received.

How difficult was it to recall the words?
Why is listening difficult?
How difficult was it not to talk without the 'stick'?

Active listening

Active listening is the technique of sifting and exploring what people are saying so that you know and they know the right message has been received and recorded. The objective is to get inside the other person's skin; to understand the situation from their perspective. It's not necessarily about solving a problem or reaching a decision. It's more to do with gaining information or creating a climate where the person can solve their own problem. It is more than just listening; as its name implies, active listening involves many very subtle responses both verbal and non-verbal.

Some of the ground rules of active listening are to:

—avoid saying you understand when you don't or when you are uncertain

—accept the right of the other person to have viewpoints which may differ from your own

—avoid jumping in with your own ideas, opinions and stories or with immediate counter-arguments or criticisms

—concentrate on listening and getting more information

—avoid probing questions that are more appropriate in push styles and rely more on open-ended questions (that can't be answered with a simple yes or no)

—try to listen to the broad ideas being mentioned and only to the detail when that becomes really necessary

—listen with your eyes and all other senses as well as just your ears, that is watch for non-verbal signals, they often include more information about the meaning of what someone is saying than the words

—avoid taking personal advantage of the information, sometimes of a personal nature, that emerges

The techniques of active listening

Paraphrasing what you hear and your understanding of the meaning
In a calm voice summarize your interpretation of what the other person has said and what they mean. Do this frequently, particularly if the other person is making a complicated point. If they are going on for a long time, break in to check your understanding and then allow them to continue. Examples are:

—'Just a minute, let me check that I have understood the first few points you are making . . .'
—'Do you mean that . . .'

Further, with paraphrasing introduce a little of your own interpretation so as to test the strength of the other person's views:

—'You are saying I should keep my voice calm, even when I'm being heavily attacked'
—'You say you are pessimistic about being able to cope with the situation even in the long term'

Reflecting feeling
Often, when you mention the feelings the other person is exhibiting you will unleash a flood of other valuable information:

—'You seem enthusiastic about the possibility'
—'You are clearly very angry'

If the response you get is a bold 'Yes' or 'No', ask if they would mind telling you a bit more.

It really doesn't matter if you have misread the feelings—the other person will usually put you right and be glad of that opportunity. Feelings misread and unchecked can cause many problems.

Arbitrary mirroring
This involves reflecting back to the other person what they have said in a way to test out the strength of that meaning. It can be particularly useful when experiencing confrontation. For example if it is said:

—'I don't believe you can be of value in this department until you have had several years' experience'

A response could be:

—'Are you saying that there is absolutely nothing I can contribute without that experience?'

Non-verbal listening
Looking people in the eye (without staring at them), nodding and making noises like 'Er', 'Um', being alert and attentive all help to demonstrate that you are indeed listening.

Active listening is one of the least costly rewards you can give someone and one of the highest marks of respect and very motivating. Because of its subtlety it is quite a difficult skill at a more sophisticated level. What matters though, as with most situations, is the underlying basic intent of the 'listener'. If you are patiently concerned to hear the other person's point of view, concentrate on that person without producing your own counter-arguments and in short give that person quality time, then the simplest level of the technique will still be productive.

10 Meetings: face to face with a group

This chapter looks at leadership in meetings and effective contributions which individuals make to group communications. At three points in the chapter suggestions are made for activities which support the text. These relate to leadership style, the pattern of meetings and seating position.

What is a meeting?

At work managers, supervisors and specialists can spend as much as a third of their time in face to face communication with two or more people. Influencing the outcome of these meetings makes a substantial contribution to a manager's performance. Successful influence depends upon preparation, the use of appropriate behavioural skills, and upon insights into some of the reasons for people's behaviour.

Meetings vary in many ways, including formality, membership, style and control and may have many different purposes. However, there are three interrelated leadership goals which need to be achieved, whatever the type of meeting. These are concerned with task, group and individual goals, which were described in the chapter on management style (*see* figure 11). For example, a meeting may have the 'task' of arriving at a solution to a problem, but may not do so if the individual members feel badly about things so that key information or advice is not given. The bad feelings may not arise if the chairman or leader can help those present to achieve their individual goals of commitment and satisfaction with the meeting. Individual feelings in turn may affect or reflect problems related to the group goals of collaboration, conflict and tension management, which again will have an impact upon the achievement of the task goals.

152

It is important that leadership is not seen as being solely the responsibility of the chairman. In many meetings there may not be a clearly established leader. Leadership is divisible. Any member of the communicating group can help the achievement of the three goals. What is it that influences effective contributions during meetings?

Effective contributions 1: planning and preparation
Leadership effectiveness during a meeting is influenced by advance preparation and reflection. The amount of time invested in this should depend upon the significance of the meeting. This is particularly important for the chairman but can also apply to members who wish to contribute to the successful outcome.

It is important not to over-prepare to the point of rigidity, so that the ability to respond to the unexpected is retained. The path to a successful meeting can be smoothed considerably by giving prior thought to the following planning checklist.

Checklist: planning meetings
WHO will or should be present?
    What positions do they hold?
    What do they know?
    What are they like?
    What do they have to gain or lose?
    What are their interpersonal or interdepartmental relations?

TIME How much?
    What can realistically be achieved in the time available?

INFORMATION What facts, figures, opinions might be needed from oneself or others?

PATHWAY Is there a logical pathway?
    Is a fixed agenda needed?
    Can a route be mapped which will allow flexibility?

PHYSICAL ARRANGEMENTS Location?
    Seating arrangements and allocation of positions?

OBJECTIVES What do you want to achieve as a result of the meeting?

TACTICS How will you influence the meeting?
    Which approaches will probably fit best?

EVENTS How does this meeting fit in with other communication events?
    Is it part of a pattern of events planned to achieve a desired outcome?

Figure 34
Communication leadership styles in meetings

DIRECTIVE			PARTICIPANT			LAISSEZ FAIRE
1	2	3	4	5	6	7
leader influences by direct or implicit reference to his power/status, rules or procedures			leader influences by 'steering' and use of skills and acceptance			leader exerts little influence upon the group
1	2	3	4	5	6	7
leader is very much the focal point of communications			leader allows frequent interaction between members			most interaction by-passes the leader
1	2	3	4	5	6	7
high proportion of messages come from the leader			other members initiate more than half the messages			other members initiate a substantial majority of messages
1	2	3	4	5	6	7
leader mainly makes statements, ie tells			leader asks a lot of questions			leader's messages are mainly questions
1	2	3	4	5	6	7
direction the meeting takes clearly controlled by leader			leader shares direction control			leader does not control direction
1	2	3	4	5	6	7
leader contributes most to the problem solving/decision making activity			leader shares problem solving/ decision making with others			leader has low influence in problem solving/decision making

Figure 34 Activity: leadership style assessment
Observe or recall a meeting which may be real or mock. Assess the leader style on the six scales above. The average score will indicate the overall style adopted. Did the style help or hinder the meeting and the achievement of the three goals: task, group, individual?
If *you* are the leader, the assessments from others of you will be interesting.

Effective contributions 2: skills, doing things which help

2(a) Communication leadership styles in meetings

Style is the pattern of communication behaviour adopted by leaders or chairmen during group communication. Styles differ according to the degree of scope allowed to other people to influence the meeting's process and outcome. A 'directive' style allows others little scope whereas a 'participant' style permits others room to influence members during a meeting. The *laissez faire*, or 'abdication' style involves allowing a free rein to the others at the meeting. A style assessment activity is suggested in figure 34 opposite.

When choosing a style, it is worth reflecting upon the effects that different approaches may have upon goal achievement and to consider the features which make up the context of the meeting. Some illustrations are also provided of this in figure 35 below.

Figure 35
Communication leadership styles: some effects and situational fit

STYLE	EFFECTS ON LEADERSHIP GOALS	SITUATION FIT
PARTICIPANT	*Task goals* Clarifies what is expected, through the encouragement of feedback Provides control information Several minds are focused on a problem, so that more ideas and information are available *Individual and group goals* Assists morale and motivation problems Members have opportunity for involvement, achievement and recognition Group has opportunity for the social rewards of collaboration	1 If members other than the leader have relevant expertise 2 If creativity is required 3 A situation of change 4 If the personal goals of members require the opportunity for involvement and recognition 5 If the commitment of members is needed 6 If group collaboration is wanted 7 If morale and motivation problems require diagnosis and action
DIRECTIVE	*Task goals* Limits the time spent on communication Limits the discretion and influence of subordinates *Individual and group goals* Provides a secure and undemanding environment Reduces the chances of conflict coming to the surface	1 If the leader is the sole source of relevant expertise 2 If there is high pressure so that the main priority is the speed of decision 3 If the personal needs of members (and the leader) require security and lack of ambiguity

2(b) Behaviour which helps the group meet its task goals

Meetings may have many different task goals or objectives, for example, problem-solving, decision-making, training or briefing. The following are types of behaviour which somebody has to produce at a meeting to help it achieve the task goals.

Initial phase
This means establishing the purpose and agenda for a meeting, agreeing how the meeting should be conducted, defining the problem and getting initial contributions from members.

Questioning
Some studies suggest that people are usually very much more willing to 'tell' than to 'ask', yet 'asking' is a vital part of leadership and is a major means of influencing what the group does. So seeking information, opinions and ideas is an important part of helping a meeting to a successful outcome.

Informing
Giving helpful information, opinions and ideas is essential as the raw material of group decision-making and problem-solving.

Clarifying
Clearing up confusion, defining terms and pointing out alternatives are necessary to help a communicating group.

Orientating
Helping the group establish where it is, where it has been and where it needs to go. This can be done by periodic summaries and by questions or suggestions about the direction to take.

Sharing
Influencing who makes contributions, inviting comments.

Deciding
Establishing a decision-making procedure, testing consensus, making a decision.

Concluding
Testing members' understanding of the conclusions and decisions,

identifying action plans—who, what, how, when. Arranging time
and place for future meetings.

2(c) Behaviour which helps the group meet individual and group goals
These are types of behaviour which help the group remain in good
working order, create a good climate for achieving task objectives
and aid the good use of members' expertise and knowledge.

Supporting
Agreeing with another person in such a way that they feel they
have been given recognition and that you are with them.

Encouraging
Helping somebody who is nervous, shy, junior in status or reluctant
to contribute to the meeting. This could mean being friendly,
warm, responsive, verbally or non-verbally.

Harmonizing
Attempting to reconcile disagreements, reducing tension; getting
people to explore their differences constructively.

Sharing
Keeping the communication channels open, getting the participation of others so that they feel involved, suggesting procedures
for sharing the available 'air time'.

Avoiding getting 'hooked'
Knowing the ways that other people can make you feel angry or
defensive and choosing not to 'take the bait'.

Assertion
Being firm and clear about what you believe or want without being
aggressive.

Constructive disagreement
Disagreeing in a way that does not upset the other person.
Incorporating other people's viewpoints into your own so that
there is constructive building. Focusing first upon what is agreed
rather than disagreed.

Contributing
Choosing to keep active and involved.

Listening
Showing verbally and non-verbally that you are paying attention to what others are saying.

Humour
Sharing humour in a way which joins the group and reduces tension. Being ready to smile or laugh with others.

Relaxation
Feeling and showing calmness and confidence. Helping others to do the same. 'Listen' to your body for tightness and tell yourself to relax. Breathe deeply if you are tense.

Helping cohesion
Helping the group to feel a team rather than a collection of indviduals. Reference to 'us' and 'we' rather than 'me', 'you' or 'I'.

Activity plan 1: meetings observation
It can be very helpful to recognize the different behaviours which help or hinder the achievement of task and climate goals at meetings.

Suggestions
Use the following two frameworks (figures 36 and 37) to observe a meeting and note the type of contributions that people make. How many of the different categories were illustrated? Were the contributions of any individuals significant for their impact upon the task or climate of the meeting?

If it is possible and agreed with your colleagues, it could be very helpful to share feedback using the framework as a guide. Use of a cassette or video recorder would provide a powerful additional aid to illustration and feedback. Remember that feedback is best given descriptively and focusing upon things that the person can do something about. It is important not to be 'judgemental', patronizing or 'superior' when giving feedback and do make sure that the individual is willing to receive it.

If members are willing, you could use a 'real' meeting for this exercise. It is, of course, possible to stage meetings for the purpose. In the latter case, encourage the members to be themselves and let them know that no Oscars will be awarded.

Possible subjects:

a) a management–union negotiation exercise

Figure 36
Meetings: task leadership

During a meeting it is important that certain 'task activities' are undertaken to take the group through to achieving its purpose. It may be one person who does this (chairman), but often it is shared by several people aware of the need.

TASK LEADERSHIP ACTIVITIES	NOTES/OBSERVATIONS
OPENING: establishing purpose and how it will be run	
INITIAL PHASE CONTRIBUTIONS: getting initial contributions from others	
QUESTIONING: seeking contributions from others	
INFORMING: giving data to others	
CLARIFYING/CONTROL: influencing the direction of the meeting, eg control questions/summaries. Where have we been, are we, should we go from here?	
ORIENTATING: indicating where the meeting has been, where it is, and where it ought to go	
SHARING: influencing who makes contributions, inviting comments	
DECIDING: bringing about a decision	
CONCLUDING: ensuring understanding, identifying future action	

b) agree a priority order of importance of the following eight jobs—
  member of Parliament
  nurse
  engineer
  dustman
  journalist
  teacher
  miner
  retailer

Figure 37
Meetings: climate leadership

Whether meetings have a successful 'task' outcome depends partly upon the 'climate'. Relationships and feelings can affect both individual contributions and the way the group works together. It may be one person who does this (chairman) but any individual member can play a part in creating or maintaining good feelings and relationships within the group.

(+)		(−)
SUPPORTING	———|———	ATTACKING
ENCOURAGING	———|———	'PUTTING DOWN'
HARMONIZING	———|———	ANTAGONIZING
SHARING OUT CONTRIBUTIONS	———|———	HOGGING 'AIR TIME'
AVOIDING GETTING 'HOOKED'	———|———	GETTING 'HOOKED'
ASSERTION	———|———	AGGRESSION
CONSTRUCTIVE DISAGREEMENT	———|———	DESTRUCTIVE DISAGREEMENT
CONTRIBUTING	———|———	WITHDRAWING
LISTENS	———|———	INTERRUPTING
HUMOUR	———|———	IMPERSONAL
RELAXED	———|———	TENSE
HELPING COHESION	———|———	CAUSING SPLITS/ DISINTEGRATION

Did any other factors help or hinder the 'climate'?

Effective contributions 3: insight, things to watch out for during a meeting

3(a) Listening to the words yet hearing the music

As in the interview, it is important during meetings to be aware of interaction processes as well as task activity. This has previously been called the words and music of face to face interaction. In figure 33 on page 138, the distinction has been made between social emotional positive and negative behaviour.

Positive behaviour indicates warmth, agreement or releases tension and is a vital element in a successful meeting. It creates a positive task climate and facilitates individual and group goal achievement.

Social emotional leadership is as important as task leadership and involves behaving in a positive way about the feelings and relationships of group members. It also requires sensitivity to

160

others, so that tensions are detected and early-warning signs of bad feelings are noticed and acted upon. Such leadership also requires an awareness of yourself and your impact upon others at a social emotional level.

The other side of the coin demands that the leader concerned about the 'music' of the meeting will try to avoid social emotional negative behaviour, which indicates unfriendliness or creates tension, for example, by 'putting down' another person. The usual pattern is for a negative act to produce a negative response from the recipient, leading to an escalation of negatives, which if not checked will mean that the words get drowned by the music.

The implication is that if an individual can remain aware of the dangers of negative escalation, it may be possible to respond in a neutral, or even positive way to a negative comment aimed at you. This could avoid the progress to conflict and perhaps disintegration.

Social emotional leadership therefore involves positive behaviour. It also requires avoiding the negative 'hook' from somebody else, however tempting the bait of conflict may often be. The effects of such insights and self control could be dramatic.

The study of group dynamics reveals the need for a balance between social emotional positive and negative behaviour in a group, so that task behaviour can be sufficient to achieve the objectives of a meeting. If there is an imbalance, it will reduce task effectiveness, and if it is not regulated, will result in disintegration of the meeting through physical or mental withdrawal (*see* figure 38 overleaf).

In figure 38 the relative proportion of the types of behaviour are only given for illustrative purposes. There is some evidence which suggests that on average social emotional positive contributions need to be at least twice those of negatives for equilibrium to be maintained. In practice, this will vary according to the group, individual personalities and the issues facing the meeting, but the general principles will apply to all group communication situations.

During the latter part of phase C, and during phase D, the leader has a number of options. One is to end the meeting, and hope that time will heal the situation. If the leader is the boss, or has power, he could invoke his authority, call the group to order and use procedure or rules to control the problem. This will not improve the social emotional climate in itself. The members may smoulder or withdraw and effective task contributions may be minimal.

Perhaps a more positive option involves actively taking the focus from the antagonists. This can be done by humour or by a summary of the meeting prior to the conflict. Movement from the area of confrontation may be achieved by judicious questioning and steering the meeting to involve other members.

A fourth option, if you operate in a sufficiently open climate of

161

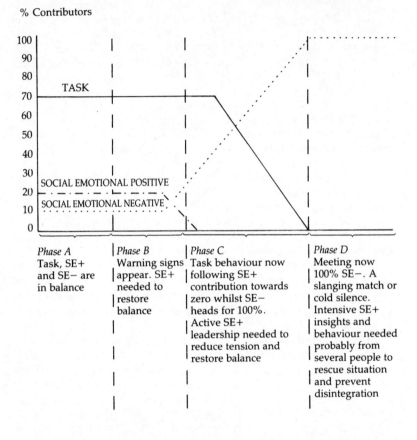

Figure 38
The relationship between task, social emotional positive and social emotional
negative behaviour at a meeting

% Contributors

Phase A
Task, SE+
and SE− are
in balance

Phase B
Warning signs
appear. SE+
needed to
restore
balance

Phase C
Task behaviour now
following SE+
contribution towards
zero whilst SE−
heads for 100%.
Active SE+
leadership needed to
reduce tension and
restore balance

Phase D
Meeting now
100% SE−. A
slanging match or
cold silence.
Intensive SE+
insights and
behaviour needed
probably from
several people to
rescue situation
and prevent
disintegration

relationships, is to explore there and then the factors which have given rise to the conflict so that they might be resolved. If this is impracticable, the causes of the difficulties may need exploring in the more confidential climate of the one to one interview.

3(b) Observing the pattern of the meeting
It can be useful to have a mental picture of the pattern of a meeting regarding who is speaking, how often and to whom. This is illustrated by the sociogram (*see* figure 39) which shows the frequency and direction of individual members' contributions at a meeting. A sociogram can be produced quite simply by 'scoring' a

meeting using a frequency and direction of comments matrix chart. An example of this is figure 40.

Activity plan 2: sociogram interpretation
In order to establish for yourself the clues that a mental picture of the frequency and direction pattern can give, it is suggested that you examine figure 39, which is derived from the scoring of a real meeting recorded in figure 40 overleaf.

Figure 39
Sociogram: frequency and direction of comments at a meeting

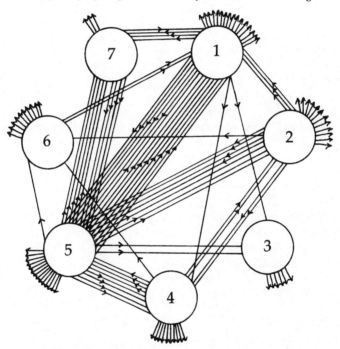

NB The arrows pointing 'out' of the group are comments made to the whole group rather than one member, ie Number 7 made three comments to the group

Can you suggest explanations of the pattern? For example, what could account for the sharing of contributions between the seven members of the meeting? Why were some high and others low? How do you interpret the direction of comments? What might explain who talked to whom; and why some members received a high proportion of comments, and some very few?

163

Can you identify the chairman? When would this sociogram be evidence of a good meeting? Similarly, when do you think it would be evidence of a bad meeting?

Figure 40
Frequency and direction of comments

| | | | COMMENTS TO | | | | | GROUP | TOTAL COMMENTS BY |
	1	2	3	4	5	6	7		
COMMENTS BY 1	×	–	1	1	5	–	3	15	25
2	3	×	–	2	4	1	–	7	17
3	–	–	×	–	2	–	–	7	9
4	–	2	–	×	4	1	–	10	17
5	8	3	2	4	×	1	5	14	37
6	2	–	–	–	–	×	–	5	7
7	1	–	–	–	4	–	×	3	8
TOTAL COMMENTS TO	14	5	3	7	19	3	8	61	120

A commentary upon the sociogram follows. It is suggested that you read this after you have produced your own interpretation.

Commentary upon the sociogram activity plan

Frequency of comments
There are many reasons for variations in frequency and direction of contributions. Not all of them are good in terms of the objects of a meeting.

One possible reason is the relative power positions of those taking part. The boss or chairman is more likely to have a high share as is a person with special expertise relevant to a meeting. Other 'highs' may be due to some individuals having a personality need to be active or to others who have personal interests to protect or promote. Interpersonal and inter-departmental conflict may also produce high scores for some participants.

A chairman adopting a participant style will score lower than one with a directive style. 'Lows' may be due to personal passivity, low interest in the proceedings, mental withdrawal as a response to attack or perceived threat or a feeling of low status in the group. A low score may also mean that the individual has primarily an information receiving role, or perhaps has nothing to say.

The 'sharing' is often not appropriate to the task objectives of a meeting. For example, an expert who is naturally reticent, and junior to others present, will remain silent and often unnoticed unless involved by other members and his vital contributions will be lost. Similarly dysfunctional will be a high share from a chairman
164

who wishes to have an 'open' discussion, or an individual with a high proportion of social emotional negative expression of conflict in his total.

In the sociogram (figure 39) Number 1 (25 comments) was the chairman. He was a chief executive who had invited his departmental heads to a meeting with the data processing manager Number 5 (37 comments) who was to present for discussion a new system. Their scores, which reflected the time spoken, were appropriate to the objectives. Number 6 (seven comments) was a systems analyst who was junior in position to all other members at the meeting. However, he was the expert who had designed the new system and might usefully have had a larger share in the proceedings. Number 4 (17 comments) was the finance manager, whose operation would be mainly affected by the change, and his proportion would seem to be about right.

Direction of comments
The interaction pattern, or who talks to whom, can be enlightening. A moving mental picture can be a valuable monitoring device for a group communication leader.

If the leader wants to use a participant style with an open exchange between all members, he would need a pattern as in figure 41 overleaf, with an even spread of comments from every member to every other member. But a directive style with the convention of addressing all comments to the chair, in a formal atmosphere, would result in a very different pattern (*see* figure 42 overleaf).

A heavy 'crossfire' or 'pairing', where interaction is focused upon two people may be constructive, or could indicate hostility and 'fighting'. Whatever the reason, it can have the effect of almost physically cutting off members from each other and acting as a barrier to interaction.

Who isn't speaking to whom may also be significant. There may be many reasons for this, but a problem could arise if, for example, two people who might spark each other off constructively and creatively fail to communicate.

An individual may receive few or no comments at all. This isolation may be dysfunctional for the group and task goals and is likely to cause some individuals to withdraw mentally.

In the sociogram the systems analyst (Number 6) was spoken to only three times. There was consequently little encouragement for him to participate. He was a very able but reticent individual. The meeting and its objectives would have been enhanced if more attempt had been made to involve him. His own boss (Number 5) only spoke to him once and the chairman (Number 1) not at all.

The purpose of the meeting in the illustration was to explain a

165

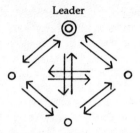

Figure 41
Participant Style

Leader

Six 'channels' possible. If all are equally used, then 16·6 per cent of messages pass through each channel. This shows a participant style. Equal sharing would mean an equal volume of messages in each direction.

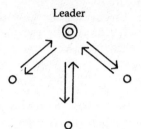

Figure 42
Directive Style

Leader

Six 'channels' possible. In this case only three are used, indicating a directive style. It would be more so if most of the messages passed from the leader to others

new system to the other members, and the chairman's role was that of facilitator to the experts. Other members needed an opportunity to discuss matters with those who had knowledge. This called for a more participant than directive style and the sociogram suggests this was the case. It also reveals that the data processing manager was the main focal point of the meeting and this was probably appropriate. However, it also reveals an inadequate role for the systems analyst, and suggests leadership faults in this instance from the chairman, data processing manager and probably others at the meeting, who could have noticed this pattern and altered it.

3(c) The impact of seating positions

Seating positions are one of the major influences on the interaction pattern of a communicating group. The relative positions and 'shape' of the group can reflect and reinforce communication styles, the degree of formality and the frequency of comments passing between individual members. It can affect the control of a meeting, social emotional relationships and the strength of individuals' feelings that they are part of a group.

Activity plan 3: seating positions

Examine the two seating plans on page 167. What should be the differences between them regarding their impact upon communi-
166

cation style; formality; frequency and direction of comments between members; control; relationships; and individuals' feelings of group identity?

If it is possible, observe meetings which use different seating plans, and note differences in the interaction patterns.

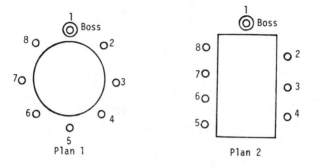

Plan 1

Plan 2

Commentary upon seating position activity

Seating plan 1

This plan suggests a democratic structure, with implicit messages of equality and uniformity, regardless of the status or rank of the members. No position has precedence in a circle. It also encourages a participant, 'all-channels' open interaction pattern for the simple, but often overlooked reason that, for people to talk readily to each other face to face, they need to be able to see each other eye to eye. Eye contact is the major cue to interaction and can easily be established with every other person in the circular system. It is more likely to result in higher feelings of group membership, and to facilitate the social emotional positive acts of encouragement and support.

Seating plan 2

This plan suggests a hierarchical structure, with the implicit message of status differences and formality. The boss is clearly in a position of precedence. It encourages a directive, 'radial' pattern of interaction, with the channels radiating from (1), the boss or chairman. Plan 2 seating arrangements have other effects that are worth considering.

The masking effect

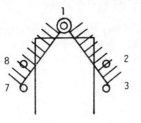

It is more difficult for the chairman (1) to establish eye contact with (2) and (8), than with other group members. They are therefore 'masked', and are less likely to be 'cued' in by the boss or to be able to cue themselves into the discussion. These may be the positions for the noisy members.

The propping effect

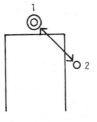

Paradoxically, positions (2) and (8) (also in the circular plan) can be the place to put a person who is nervous or shy in group situations. If the boss is sufficiently nurturing and conscious of the need, physically close proximity and the supportive nuances of voice tone and eye contact can help 'prop' the shy individual, and can encourage confidence and contributions.

Physically close proximity can encourage confidence and contributions.

The crossfire and shielding effect

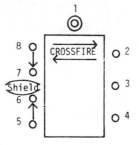

If the boss/chairman uses a participant approach, and allows interaction which by-passes him, there is likely to be a high

There is likely to be a high frequency of contact between people sitting opposite each other.

frequency of contact between people sitting opposite each other. This again will result from the ease of eye contact cues. The message from this is clear, if you want two people to talk with each other. It is equally clear that if you want to avoid destructive

It is much more difficult to sustain hostile exchanges from these positions.

169

negative crossfire, don't place two people who have personal animosity or a conflict of interests opposite each other. To reduce the chances of such battles, the best positions for the potential antagonists will be (5) and (8), where they are mutually shielded physically by (6) and (7). Experiment or observation will reveal that it is much more difficult to sustain hostile exchanges from these positions.

The anchor man effect

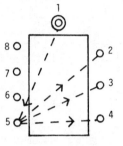

If you hope to share your task or social emotional leadership with others at the meeting, or to have others help you control it and especially if you think it will be stormy, you will need to place them in the anchor man positions. These are (4) and (5), which are the optimum strategic eye-contact positions. They are the easiest for the chairman to cue in, and in turn are well placed for eye-contact and verbal exchanges with other group members.

Some people are intuitively aware of the significance of the seating positions they choose. Those who wish to avoid another will sit out of eye-contact with that person. Those who want to fight another will sit opposite their opponents. Others who wish to dominate will choose (1), or if that is the boss, then they will choose the anchor positions (4) and (5).

3(d) Problem solving meetings: keeping in step
It is not unusual for problem solving meetings to generate a disproportionate amount of confusion, which has its impact on both task achievement (getting a good solution) and the feelings of the group members. This confusion often stems from individuals operating at different phases of the problem solving process at the same time.

Many difficulties can be avoided if the group's leadership can steer the meeting systematically through each problem phase, helping the members to be aware of the stage they are at.

The first phase is *problem awareness*, when the group recognizes

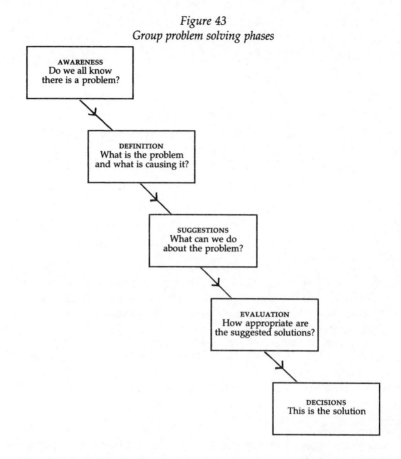

Figure 43
Group problem solving phases

AWARENESS
Do we all know
there is a problem?

DEFINITION
What is the problem
and what is causing it?

SUGGESTIONS
What can we do
about the problem?

EVALUATION
How appropriate are
the suggested solutions?

DECISIONS
This is the solution

that something requires a solution. This is followed by the *definition* phase, which establishes the nature of the problem and a diagnosis of its causes. It is at this point that difficulties often arise in the group. Agreement amongst members about the reasons for a problem is often assumed, rather than tested, and the different perceptions which may exist can create conflict later. Some group members are frequently reluctant to dwell at this phase and move rapidly ahead to making solution *suggestions*. Once more, some members may not wait for suggestions to be explained or clarified before they proceed with the evaluation phase.

Small wonder, if members of the group are scattered over different phases of the process, that the decision or solution point is difficult to reach without confusion or conflict. It is a part of the leader's job to help the group keep in step through the different phases of the problem solving process.

11 Work groups: managing performance and relationships

The first section of this chapter has a number of linked elements which develop a theme about work groups and performance. Alongside the theme is an activity plan which asks the reader to do or think about things related to each element of the theme. You may wish to complete the activity plan with written work, simply reflect upon the questions or carry out simple behavioural experiments and observations.

The second section is the text, which may be read independently from the activity plan. The text is an expansion of the theme in section one but is not intended to provide the right answer to the questions posed. However, you will find it useful to relate it to your own thinking.

Introduction

A manager judges himself and is judged by others. One basis for these judgements is the performance of the work groups and individuals who work for him. Management means the achievement of results through other people.

Everybody who has experienced work organizations will be able to recall collections of people who could be identified as a work group. For the purpose of examining the management of performance, we shall assume that we are discussing a *subordinate work group*. The group will have a fairly permanent nucleus of individuals; members' jobs will be linked and are perhaps similar or identical. They will have the same boss, and are likely to have many other things the same, such as payment, conditions, location and grievances. Individuals will probably need to collaborate with other group members, will have fairly frequent face to face contact with them and feel that they have a lot in common. The manager would do well not to ignore the significance and strengths of work groups.

172

Theme and activity plan

THEME	ACTIVITY PLAN
All organizations have *control systems* to influence the job performance of individual members	What can an individual contribute to job performance?
MANAGEMENT'S PERFORMANCE CONTROL SYSTEM consists of: (a) *Rewards* A reward is something available to an individual as a result of his membership of an organization and what he does at work. It is anything that meets a personal 'need' or 'want'. These needs could by physical, security, social, reputation, self esteem or self fulfilment	What rewards to an individual can be influenced by management?
(b) *Standards* These are the basis for assessing an individual's or group's performance. In theory, the rewards ensure that management's standards are met, because better performance yields better rewards	What can make it difficult to establish standards and assess performance?
(c) *Management hierarchy* These are the different levels through which the management performance control system is administered and monitored	
Management does not possess the only performance control system, although it sometimes wishes and often acts as if it did. There is usually a parallel system based upon the work group equals and colleagues of an individual WORK GROUP PERFORMANCE CONTROL SYSTEM consists of: (a) *Rewards*	What rewards are available from equals/colleagues at work?
(b) *Standards (group norms)* Group norms are the unwritten standards of behaviour and performance that a group expects from its individual members. By conforming to the norms, the individual gets rewards. Not conforming may result in 'punishment' from the group!	What aspects of behaviour and performance are subject to influence by group norms? Can you identify the norms of any group to which you belong? You might try deliberately breaking a norm (the authors accept no responsibility for the result!) What does it feel like? How did others in the group react? Why do groups have norms?

THEME	ACTIVITY PLAN
(c) *Group hierarchy* Most work groups develop an unofficial 'pecking order'. Although everybody in a group may be at the same level and even doing the same job, some individuals exert more influence over the group than others. This is sometimes called informal or 'natural' leadership	Observe or reflect upon a group you know well. Can you map out the 'pecking order'? Who are the leaders? What makes them leaders? How do they exercise their influence? Is there more than one type of leader?
As outlined, there are two performance control systems influencing individuals at work. One is based upon management, the other on the work group. This can be called the dual control system	Comparing the two systems, how might they conflict with each other so that problems develop for management?
One management problem resulting from the dual control system could be the performance gap. This is when management's standards of performance are higher than the group norms One way of representing the performance gap is:	

Figure 33

The performance gap

High performance ... (MS) ... ? individual ... Low performance (GN)	Management standards supported by management rewards
	Are most people likely to be closer to MS or GN? What kind of person is likely to be closer to MS? What kind of person is likely to be closer to GN?
group norms supported by group rewards	Supposing most people in a group are nearer to the group norm than management standard. Can you produce an approach and a list of things that management could do to positively influence group performance?
The individual is being pulled towards MS by the management control system and to GN by the group control system	

Individuals and job performance

An individual's contribution to job performance will vary from job to job. In some cases physical abilities and effort will be most important; in others mental aptitude will have greater significance;

174

others again will place most demand upon skill in personal relationships and so on.

What does influence performance at work? There is no doubt that individuals bring to the job their own ideas about a 'fair day's work' and control performance according to their own standards. This can be called the 'conscience' factor, and perhaps in an ideal world organizations could rely upon this as the only means of achieving appropriate performance levels. In recent years some organizations have attempted to place increasing emphasis upon an individual's responsibility for his own work standards. Management by objectives, job enrichment, autonomous work groups and participation can be seen as moves in this direction.

No organization relies exclusively on the conscience factor and all have control systems to influence the level of performance of their members. The management of performance requires an understanding of performance control systems, which have three main elements:

rewards — standards — hierarchy

Management's performance control system

Management rewards
These are given to subordinates in return for their membership of the organisation and their performance measured against the standards expected by the management hierarchy.

Rewards
These are not just material things. They are anything which meets an active need of an individual or group. A punishment, conversely, is anything which prevents a need from being met.

For example, if you have a need to enhance your self-esteem, praise from a respected boss could meet it, and hence would be a 'reward' which could encourage a repeat of the performance which produced it.

In this sense, many things could be rewards in management's control system. Money, fringe benefits, working conditions, job interest, responsibility, promotion, recognition, praise and status symbols are some of them.

Management standards
These are the basis for assessing whether performance has been good, average or bad from management's viewpoint. Some jobs can be 'measured' by work study, such as repetitive tasks requiring mainly physical skills. Similarly, some aspects of job behaviour,

175

such as timekeeping, can be recorded accurately. Even in these cases, when 'measurement' is possible, there is great scope for disagreement about whether the amount or quality you have measured is 'good' or 'bad'. You have probably seen ice-skating or gymnastic championships on television and observed the frequent disparity between judges' scores. This often seems to happen when a judge is scoring a performance from a compatriot—when scores tend to be higher—or a compatriot's main rival—when scores tend to be lower. The competitors themselves would no doubt rate themselves differently again. There is a 'subjective' element in all standard setting and assessment.

Whatever the problems of subjectivity and measurement, managers do set standards, develop means of assessment and gather 'evidence' about subordinates' performance. They shouldn't be surprised if the subordinates disagree with their opinions about how good or bad that performance is. 'Facts', if they can be gathered, rather than opinions are an important aid to agreement.

The management hierarchy
This administers and monitors the rewards, standards and performance in the control system which is sometimes explicit and designed for the purpose. But most often, it is implicit and has evolved in a piecemeal fashion.

Management often assumes that its performance control system is the only one operating in an organization. This often leads to inadequate diagnosis of performance problems and hence ineffective solutions, because it has failed to take into account another performance control system within the organization: that based upon the work group, which excludes the management hierarchy.

The work group's performance control system

Group rewards
These are given to individual members by their 'equals' or colleagues in return for conforming to *group standards* or *norms*, which are expectations that the group has about individual behaviour and performance. This process is monitored by a group hierarchy or informal leadership. *Group rewards* are such things as friendship, acceptance as a member, support and cooperation, recognition and respect from colleagues in the subordinate group.

Group norms
These can govern all the important aspects of job performance, including output, quality, cooperation with management or other
176

groups, time-keeping and absenteeism. These standards are rarely written down or consciously learned but new members rapidly learn what is expected from them. Non-conformity to the group norms will produce a reaction from other members ranging from humorous rebukes to severe social pressure and the withholding of group rewards. Most people are dependent in some respect upon their colleagues in the group so its sanctions are powerful.

Group norms do not exist through some perverse law of cussedness in order to restrict individual freedom or make management's life difficult, although they may appear to do both things. Norms have the function of making relationships more predictable and less ambiguous. They are also often seen to protect or promote the interests of the group.

The group hierarchy is the informal 'pecking-order', sometimes known as 'natural leadership'. These are individuals who do not have managerial or supervisory positions but who exercise influence within the group, and may 'represent' the group to management or other groups.

Relations between natural leaders and groups vary considerably. In some cases the leader is able to dominate and to define the norms; in others his own role and behaviour are governed by them. Some leaders are easily noticed by their actions and words, but it would be wrong to assume that these are necessarily the most influential or significant people in the group. Often a 'quieter' member will prepare the case and decide the strategy for the more vocal member to present for the group. Sometimes the group will have a 'policeman' who monitors the norms and a 'judge' who indicates how the group should react to the norm-breaker. Another type of informal leader is the 'exemplar' who makes no attempts to dominate the group but whose opinions are highly valued and define the group norms.

Management problems and the dual control system
Many problems for management, groups and individuals can arise because of conflict between the two control systems.

Conflict between management and group rewards can occur. For example, an individual may be torn between a desire to gain the reward of promotion and the need to keep the friendship of his work colleagues. In some cases, for example, if he performs to management standards this will help him get his advancement but at the same time may lead to rejection by his group colleagues, who could expect very different attitudes and behaviour.

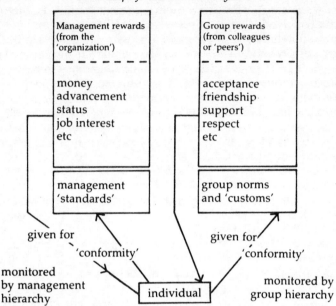

Figure 45
The dual performance control system

There are two performance control systems in organizations, one based upon management, the other upon the work group.

Conflict can occur between the management hierarchy and group 'natural leaders' over power and influence within the work group.

Conflict of perception based upon management and group values is commonplace. For example, a manager may believe an informal leader to be a bloody-minded troublemaker whose main aim is disruption. On the other hand the group leader may believe he is legitimately leading the group to protect its interests against the exploitation attempts of the manager.

A 'good worker' from management's viewpoint may be rejected by the group because he doesn't conform to the norms of the group.

A 'performance gap' problem will occur if there is a marked difference between management standards and group norms of performance (*see* figure 45). In this case, the two control systems are pulling the individual in opposite directions.

178

The dual control system and the performance gap

When an individual is being pulled in opposite directions, he often resolves the conflict by withdrawing from the situation, either by absenteeism or leaving.

If he stays and is in a weak group, values management's rewards more than the group's, has an individualistic approach to work or is content to be an isolate, then he will probably approximate more to management's performance standards than the group's.

If he is in a strong and cohesive group, values the group's rewards or needs to be accepted by his colleagues, then he will probably conform to the group norms (*see* figure 46).

Figure 46
Factors affecting group cohesion and rewards

COHESION AND REWARDS (+)	FACTORS	COHESION AND REWARDS (−)
fit	personalities	clash
positive	relationships	negative
accepted	group leadership	rejected
close	proximity of colleagues	distant
team	task activity	individual
frequent	opportunities for social contacts	limited
long	duration of membership	short
high	acceptance of internal differences	low
high	felt common interests	low

Management approaches to the performance gap

The dual control system and performance gap defines many problems that management has to solve. There is a two stage approach that can be taken towards a solution; diagnostic and action.

Diagnostic Stage

This is really saying 'think before you act'. First of all define the problem. What are management standards? What are the group norms? How big is the gap? What do you know about the reward systems? Secondly, diagnose the causes of the problem. Why is there a gap? How are management standards set? Why are the group norms what they are?

This 'finding out' stage is important and often seems to be forgotten, sometimes with disastrous results. It would be the same if doctors attempted to prescribe medicine or surgery without prior diagnosis.

Finding out means seeking information from and about the group. It involves understanding the group members and what takes place between them. Identifying and establishing a relationship with the natural leaders is another essential aid to a diagnosis of the performance gap problem. However vital this diagnosis stage is, it is equally important not to succumb to the disease of 'analysis paralysis'. Once the problem is clearer and the causes are emerging, the action stage has been reached.

Action Stage

What sort of options are available to the manager? There are four broad approaches which might have an impact upon group performance (figure 47):

lowering management standards
outbidding the group—improving management rewards
outbidding the group—weakening the group control system
raising group norms—harnessing the group control system.

1 *Lowering management standards*

At first glance this may appear a defeatist policy from management's viewpoint, serving only to hide rather than tackle the performance problem. This could be true. It has frequently been observed that some organizations have progressively lowered their performance expectations. Some have experience showing that group norms may fall in proportion, so that the gap is never closed and performance declines.

This is not the whole story. Experienced managers have often noticed that unrealistically high standards, which can't be reached, are very demoralizing. This can result in the group establishing very low norms as a defence. Setting more realistic standards, perhaps with a downward adjustment, may have the effect of encouraging a higher level of performance from groups and individuals. The way managers arrive at their standards will also be significant. Involvement of the group in standards setting could lead to a convergence of management standards and group norms.

180

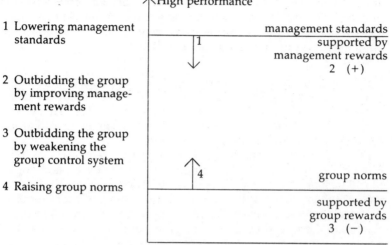

Figure 47
Management approaches to the performance gap

High performance

1 Lowering management
standards

2 Outbidding the group
by improving manage-
ment rewards

3 Outbidding the group
by weakening the
group control system

4 Raising group norms

management standards
supported by
management rewards
2   (+)

1

group norms

supported by
group rewards
3   (−)

4

2 *Outbidding the group—improving management rewards*

Essentially this approach means making management rewards so attractive to individuals in the group that they prefer these to group rewards, and are more likely to 'break' the norms. Some motivational strategies are designed to do just this, individual piece rate payment systems being a prime example. The problem is that such approaches encourage an individualistic competitive attitude and often reduce cooperation and encourage conflict. The improvement of promotion prospects, status and methods of creating job interest and involvement are all approaches that may work in some situations, but they all suffer from two disadvantages. They tend to be expensive and in continuous need of improvement. Secondly, they do not make use of the strong influence of the group control system; rather, they seek to minimize the influence of the group.

3 *Outbidding the group—weakening the group control system*

Even more than the previous approach, this tries to minimize group influence by directly attacking the group's means of control. This could entail breaking up the group or redesigning group members' work so that there is little opportunity for 'exchanging' rewards. It attempts to reduce group cohesion by creating the negative factors mentioned earlier (*see* figure 46 on page 179) so that the group is destroyed, leaving only management's control and reward system to influence individual performance.

181

This may sound attractive to the Machiavellian manager, but even in his terms there are many probable costs that are likely to make this approach ineffective. It could lead to the development of anti-management norms, long term mistrust and lowering morale. There is also evidence that when group reward opportunities decline, absenteeism and labour turnover increase. In addition, it neglects the productive potential of the group.

4 Raising group norms—harnessing the group control system

The aim of this approach is to reduce the performance gap by raising group norms towards management standards. This would harness group control and mean that both management and group systems are pulling in the same direction.

Before describing some ways of attempting to raise group norms, it is important to restate that norms are not the easy plaything of Machiavellian management. All the evidence suggests that norms are only likely to change when the group, or significant members of it, feel that the change will protect or promote the group interest. These are the purposes that norms serve and there will be no real progress if members feel they will not be met. What approaches could harness the group system?

Joint standard setting. Involve the natural leader, group representatives or, if it is small enough, the whole group in the standard setting activity. At the very least, identify the performance gap and discuss it and if possible consider how it could be narrowed. If it can be achieved, full involvement in arriving at an agreed decision can be most productive. This is what many organizations do on a one-to-one basis with management by objectives (MbO) and the principle can apply equally to groups.

Not many years ago most managers would have felt emasculated if they adopted a group participation approach. The cry of 'we will not abdicate managerial responsibilities' is heard less often as the backwoods disappear and the last bastions of exclusive managerial prerogative fall to the realities of the last decades of the twentieth century. The modern management ego appears less threatened by the concept of joint decision making.

Of course, this joint approach may well call for bargaining. The negotiation of a compromise between management performance standards and group norms is what effective productivity bargaining is all about. It involves management and the group agreeing in detail upon the new standards and the price to be paid to protect and promote the group interests.

Participation methods such as 'briefing groups' and 'quality circles' may assist 'joint standard setting' and help close the gap between group norms and management standards. Briefing groups
182

provide a built-in reminder to managers to keep people 'in the picture' about significant matters and encourage discussion. This may prevent the development of norms which prevent the group performing to the manager's expectations. Quality circles techniques, which may be adapted in a number of forms to suit the need of the situation, have much potential for addressing some of the negative norms or low performance problems. In these forms they may be led by the manager or a member of the work group; they may be voluntary or seen as part of the work rôle involving everyone; they may concentrate on quality issues or be much wider. What is common however is a structured approach to joint problem solving and if successful the performance gap will be narrowed.

Influencing norms through natural leaders. If you subscribe to the 'troublemaker' theory of conflict, you could be tempted to remove the natural leader from the scene in the belief that that person is responsible for holding down the group norm. The tactics vary from promoting to sacking the 'troublemaker', or possibly transferring to another department the problems you feel are being created.

There is common experience that if you choose your person wisely, the 'poacher turned gamekeeper' promotion can be very effective. However there are often limitations to the troublemaker theory. In the first place they may only reflect or represent the group feeling, not determine it. Remove them in a way that is seen to be manipulative and the problem will get worse. The chances are that your troublemaker is only a symptom not a cause of the performance gap and related difficulties. Another will probably take that person's place and the situation may be worse than before. The fact that group norms are often stronger than a group leader could also present a problem. If the 'natural leader' changes as a result of discussion or influence she may well have put herself upon a limb, which the group will cut off. 'Natural' leadership is rarely natural and everlasting! Leadership is often conditional upon the leader herself conforming to norms.

This approach can be effective but it seems to rely upon a relationship of trust and openness between formal leader (manager/supervisor) and natural leader, which does not prejudice the latter's position in the group. If he or she is really respected as a person of integrity by the group and comes to accept the real advantages of a different norm, there is a good prospect of success. The manager will need to accept, when using this approach, that the natural leader may influence the manager's own view of appropriate standards. The modifications may need to be mutual.

Influencing norms through management style. All managers develop a style or regular pattern of behaviour and relationships towards

183

Influencing Norms: the 'poacher turned gamekeeper' promotion can be very effective.

others. It is probable that this is one of the most critical factors in developing strong and productive teams sharing common goals. A style which fits a group and its circumstances could positively influence group norms and close the performance gap.

How do you know your own style? And if you know what it is, how do you know if it fits your situation? This is something which was explored in detail in chapter two.

Relationships between groups
In addition to managing a group's performance a manager could have problems with relationships between groups which could hinder the achievement of the organization's objectives. It often happens that groups become incredibly committed to their own goals and norms and, particularly if the organization has a competitive climate, this may lead to conflict between groups which can be very unproductive with reduced collaboration or even hostility. All the group control pressures described earlier in the chapter will influence individual members to adopt conflict behaviour and attitudes towards the other group.

We have probably all attended meetings or know of organizations where rivalry for resources or for the adoption of a particular course of action has been intense. At such meetings members take on the role of representatives for their department or group and only to a much reduced extent that of a member of the total organization concerned to find the best organizational solution to a problem. In the light of the pressures on such 'representatives' this is not surprising. Here the individual is locked into a rôle so he is not able to change his mind independently on the basis of fresh evidence. Rather, if he alters his thinking from that of his group and gives way to another point of view, he is likely to be perceived by them as a 'traitor'.

184

If on the other hand he is able to persuade the other groups to his group's thinking, he will be regarded by his own group as a 'hero'. There are too those organizations where rivalry between groups or departments is such that in essence the organization consists of a number of 'fiefs' or 'robber barons'.

The effects of this may occur in complex and subtle ways, such as making a private decision not to do something, as when one department knows another has made a minor error and lets it build up to a major one so they are seen to have dropped a 'clanger'. Another way is giving false information or withholding information to score over a rival group. These are difficult for the organization to control by edict: they depend on the relationships between groups.

Handling intergroup conflict
1 *Common overriding goals*
   If the manager can help both groups to see that they have common goals, it will help collaboration. This will be reinforced if it is demonstrated that both groups will gain by working together.
2 *Creating a third group*
   It could be helpful to create a third group consisting of exemplars or high prestige members of the two groups to work on a task for mutual benefit. This may produce new norms and perception of the other group which are more collaborative. It is important that the joint task is one which does not simply reinforce the 'us' and 'them' feelings.
3 *Job rotation*
   One of the many benefits of job rotation is that, through experience in a number of departments, people tend to become broader in outlook and able to understand and tolerate more the views of other groups.
4 *Increasing contact*
   It may be possible for the manager to increase positive contact between two conflicting groups, perhaps by social or sports activities. 'In-house' training, where members from different groups attend the same course, has often been shown to break down inter-group barriers.

12 Managing change

In the first section of this chapter the way in which organizations need to be adaptive in order to survive is explored and the management of change examined as a process. Several 'thinking tools' are discussed and examples of their use given. In the second section there are a number of activities designed to allow you to test out these 'tools' and to gain a greater insight into your attitudes to innovation.

We live in a world of change, and one where the rate of change is increasing rapidly. We only need to consider the amount of change that has occurred within our grandparents', parents', and our own lifetimes for this to be strikingly illustrated. Such change has been both technological and social and has had a marked impact not only on society at large but within the workplace.

It has been argued that, despite man's largely successful adaptation to the many changes that have confronted him, the rate of change is increasing so rapidly that, at some future date not so far off, change will occur so rapidly and with such intensity that it will cause the phenomenon of 'future shock'. Future shock is a term coined to describe the effects on people if change occurs at such a rate that they are unable to assimilate it. It is one, projected, view of what could result if the rate of change continues to accelerate. It explains too why many see the forces of 'conservative dynamism', that is the effort applied to maintain a *status quo*, as being strong and active, particularly within working organizations.

In recent years the rate of change has accelerated to a point where 'discontinuities' have become increasingly frequent, that is change is evident not just as a gradual process, whatever the pace, but as an abrupt transition, often without precedent, to a new situation, whether that situation be markets, products, career patterns or whatever. Thus the need to manage 'quantum' rather
186

than 'incremental' change has become more acute for sheer business survival. Quantum change can only be supported and implemented well in an organization that has developed a culture to support it. Likewise quantum change as experienced in personal career terms needs an underlying capacity to adjust successfully. It is said that today's manager will need to make four or so major career shifts over the next 20 years or so of his career. The capacity to deal successfully with change then not only matters at the level of managing the organization and its success, but also at the individual level for managers in terms of their personal career.

It can certainly be said that change within the working environment is often difficult to manage. Frequently this is not so much due to the technical component of the change but to the way people react to it. The greatest factor in change is human. Important things to people, like career paths, known working habits, the use of prized skills and relationships with others, may be threatened. In some companies and in some cultures the word 'change' itself has negative overtones.

A central skill in management, and many would argue the central skill, is in inducing and managing that change needed for successful business positioning and success. It is unlikely that this will be a one-off process, but rather a continuous one. Part of this central skill is the smooth introduction of change or, putting it another way, 'overcoming resistance to change'. Some managers may deride what they see as emotional or illogical factors concerning people's reactions to, say, a technical change but if they do so they are likely to be less successful in implementing change smoothly.

The socio-technical system
Change is therefore likely to affect not only the way a job is done but also the response of those who will perform it, and it is evident that there will be interaction between these two. The first stage in the successful management of change is to use a suitable framework to analyze and understand how the various factors involved in change impact one upon another, and thus predict and control the consequences. The socio-technical systems concept provides such a framework.

The idea behind the concept is that there are three major elements or systems that make up an organization: the technical system, the formal social system and the informal social system, each of which are interrelated so that changes in one system will induce changes in the others. The whole make up the total so called socio-technical system. The technical system refers to the methods, practices, procedures, techniques and technology employed for processing the work. These will obviously vary between different kinds of

187

organizations—banking, manufacturing, retailing or whatever—and between departments in an organization such as production and research.

The technical system is of course operated by people who are organized within the formal social system, which is concerned with such factors as the organization structure, the designated management hierarchy, span of control, formal communication networks and role specialization. The relationship between the formal social system and the technical system was graphically demonstrated by Joan Woodward's classic study which examined the type of organization, its structure, technology and operation in over 100 firms. It seems self-evident today that a clear correlation exists between technical complexity and features of the formal social organization such as the number of levels in the hierarchy, the span of control, the flexibility of the structure and the communication system. Yet before 1958 it was assumed, by classical management theorists at least, that any organization irrespective of its technology was best organized according to one set of principles.

Obviously an appropriate formal social system will reflect the characteristics of the technical system employed: an appropriate formal social system for a small jobbing shop will clearly be different from that employed in a large-scale process industry such as an oil refinery. Thus any change in the technical system may require, and often does, a change in the formal social system.

As any experienced manager is only too well aware, the formal social system rarely operates effectively without the active support and goodwill of staff. This can be vividly illustrated by the extreme situation of 'working to rule'. Even under less extreme circumstances the degree of active support and goodwill enlisted has a great effect on the success of the organization, although the formal social system seeks to regulate and control behaviour. The third of the interdependent systems is the informal social system. This is concerned with such factors as attitudes, motivation, relationships and behaviour which individuals and groups adopt at work, and is a crucial part of the socio-technical system.

Thus the three elements in the socio-technical system are significantly related to one another so that, for example, the technical system is very likely to influence the nature of the formal social system and the types of behaviour displayed in the informal social system. Equally, it is possible that, through the expression of certain types of attitudes and behaviours, the informal social system may affect the other systems, such as adaptations to the organization structure and the methods employed for performing tasks. The interdependence of the systems that comprise the total socio-technical system is shown in figure 48.

More recently, the effect of what is known as corporate 'culture'

188

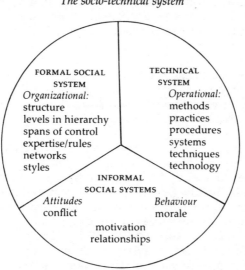

Figure 48
The socio-technical system

FORMAL SOCIAL
SYSTEM
Organizational:
structure
levels in hierarchy
spans of control
expertise/rules
networks
styles

TECHNICAL
SYSTEM
Operational:
methods
practices
procedures
systems
techniques
technology

INFORMAL
SOCIAL SYSTEMS
Attitudes
conflict

Behaviour
morale

motivation
relationships

in the effectiveness or otherwise of companies has come to be widely recognized. Culture can be seen as 'the way things are done around here'. What came out of a study of several 'excellent' organizations which had managed to prosper well over a considerable period of time through constant adaptation was the importance of the so-called 'soft aspects', that is the informal social systems, part of the integrated whole in providing the necessary mechanisms for continuous adaptation. Factors such as style, skills, superordinate goals, informal communication systems, staff, etc can in fact be observed directly, even measured. It is suggested that these variables are at least as important as strategy and structure in orchestrating major change; indeed they are critical for achieving necessary or desirable change. A characteristic of culture is that it tends to be all-pervasive and enduring, and often the major step in promoting significant change is focused at the culture itself initially. Changes in strategy and structure, on the surface, may happen quickly, but they are likely to be only superficial unless there is fundamental and real absorption of them within the informal social system. The pace of real change then is geared to all these variables and those companies who have over the years generated a culture that is prepared for major change will be those able to adapt quickly and effectively to it.

The value of the socio-technical concept in terms of managing change is that it provides a logical framework for examining

189

whether changes in one system may have significant influences and repercussions in the others. This can be extremely useful when planning and developing change or innovation. As a further illustration the following change case, which concerned a major retailing organization, draws together many of the points:

The company operated three retail outlets which were located in different suburbs of a major city. Each outlet had its own adjoining warehouse where stock was kept and issued to the outlet on demand. The system had worked well for several years.

For sound economic reasons such as to reduce staff levels, transport and distribution costs and working capital tied up in stock, the company decided to rationalize its warehousing operation by building a new purpose designed and centralized warehouse, about two miles from each outlet, which was to service all the three outlets in the city. Although the expected savings in the warehousing part of the operation materialized, there was some loss of sales at the outlets and also morale decreased appreciably at both the warehouse and the outlets.

In the previous technical system the ordering and transfer of stock from its warehouse to an outlet was achieved through a simple paperwork system. Issue was generally achieved within half an hour and the system was flexible enough to deal with small quantities. Stock levels were agreed weekly between the outlet manager and the warehouse manager responsible to him. Within overall guidelines the outlet manager was allowed much discretion as to the amount and type of stock ordered, so he was able to cater for local trading patterns.

When the centralized warehouse was introduced stock ordering and control was carried out by headquarters. Deliveries were made by van four times a day to the retail outlets for orders placed at least four hours earlier and authorized by the floor supervisor. Minimum quantities were also laid down. These were some of the changes made to the technical system and, because of them, it was necessary to modify the formal social system of organizational structure, roles etc. Previously a warehouse manager was responsible to an outlet manager; now the one warehouse manager was responsible to the district office.

One of the previous warehouse managers was put in charge of the new system, another became his assistant and the third left the company under a voluntary redundancy scheme, as did one-third of the other warehouse staff. The roles of staff in the new system were more specialized in that staff dealt only with a prescribed range of stock instead of serving a store in total. These changes in the formal social system flowed from the

190

changes in the technical system. However, both had effects on the informal social system which were largely not expected.

As far as the retail assistants were concerned they had had previously direct and face-to-face contact with the warehouse staff. Also, under the informal communications network system that had grown up, they were able to telephone warehouse staff directly and arrange for small orders to be processed. This had the effect of maintaining appropriate stock levels despite day to day fluctuations, avoided delays when supervisors were busy and induced a high level of commitment, identity and morale. The warehouse staff also had a high identity with the outlet, responded to the informal communication system and had a high level of morale. As well as having a productive and satisfying relationship with the sales staff, they operated as friendship groups and also welcomed the degree of variety and autonomy in their roles.

Under the new arrangement sales staff had no direct contact with warehouse staff except in the person of the van driver and all orders had to be processed through the supervisors. As well as restricting the degree of autonomy and control they had enjoyed, it meant that there was less 'fine tuning' in stock levels, and consequently more items were out of stock or understocked than previously.

The impact of the new approach on the warehouse staff resulted in several major changes in the informal social system. No longer being in direct contact with the sales floors of the outlets, they had less commitment and identity towards them. The new technical and formal social systems were found to be impersonal and allowed less variety and responsibility in their roles. They were also concerned about a possible further reduction in manning levels, and took care to work strictly to the system laid down instead of, as before, developing informal ways to facilitate it. In the previous situation they had operated largely in autonomous and friendship groups; now they worked within tightly prescribed roles. Promotional opportunities were also perceived to be less good, and some of the staff found that getting to their new place of work was much more inconvenient. It is not surprising that morale and commitment, previously at a high level, had declined severely. Yet the effects of changes in the informal social system could have been planned for and controlled. It is not untypical for a great deal of effort to be invested in planning changes in the technical and formal social systems, but relatively little thought given to consequences on the informal social system.

Another example which illustrates the interrelationship of the technical, formal social and informal social systems occurred in a freezing works where goods were despatched in container lorries.

Most loads were palletized and handled by fork-lift truck; however, some were irregular in shape and could not be palletized or stacked mechanically; although bulky, they had instead to be manhandled the length of the container. The despatch manager was concerned that not only was the system inefficient but that it also placed undue physical stress on the loading crew.

After spending some time considering ways to make improvements he eventually decided to use flexible conveyor track. He was able to convince his management that his proposal was a sound one and the equipment was purchased and installed. But, the system worked even less efficiently than the previous one. This the manager found difficult to understand as all his calculations had indicated otherwise. The reasons for the disappointing results became clear when he examined what had happened.

In the changed system of work organization one man was stationed at the end of the conveyor, working by himself within the container. The pace of the operation was thus controlled by this one man. The loading gang had previously worked as a group, and there had been a group pace about the work. Further, they were a group of immigrant Italians for whom group working and close contact fitted their cultural norms. This was too the pattern outside the work place; they lived in close proximity and their wives visited each other regularly. The new work organization had had the effect of breaking up the group pattern of work and the close contact with other members of the group that it had provided. This was experienced particularly strongly by the operator stationed at the end of the track in the depths of the container, and his response to being isolated was reflected in his work rate. Once the manager realized what was happening he was able to rearrange the work organization to take such factors into account, and the efficiency of the new system quickly reached the level he had planned.

These two cases demonstrate the inter-relationship of the systems within an organization that make up the socio-technical system. To complete the picture it is necessary to look not only within the organization but also outside it and therefore at the external environment in which it operates.

The external environment
An organization is not a closed system but is subject to influences such as markets, changes in technology, government policies etc

in the environment in which it operates. Patently, to regard an organization as closed instead of being to some degree open to its environment is a recipe for non-survival. Some writers on management argue that the primary task of senior management is to monitor and manage the boundaries between the organization and the environment in which it operates. Often change is induced from outside the organization and requires necessary adaptation within it to ensure survival. Examples of this over recent years have been the exploitation of computer technology, automation, market changes such as the movement away from canned to frozen vegetables, changes in expectations people have about the way they are to be treated and managed, and the growth of white collar trade unionism. To regard change as a necessary adaptation to ensure the survival of the organization is a useful perspective, particularly when considering implementation and communication strategies.

Environments in which organizations operate range from those that are relatively stable to those that are subject to rapid change (dynamic) or even turbulent. There is an increasing tendency for the environment to become more and more dynamic, in that it is subject to rapid change, or even turbulent in that it is unpredictable and has many conflicting aspects. To cope successfully the organization must be sufficiently flexible to adapt and have appropriate structures and systems in order to manage the change. As the environment becomes increasingly dynamic or turbulent so that there is less certainty, a greater stress inevitably will be placed on a manager's 'tolerance of ambiguity', and on his 'resourcefulness' in dealing with hitherto unknown situations. It is possible that many people may experience the lack of certainty inherent in rapid change as threatening and stressful. Yet if survival through successful adaptation is to be achieved, the 'resistance to change' defence mechanisms some people employ for their own psychological security will have to be coped with.

One of the difficulties arising when change becomes more rapid is that it involves breaking down or un-learning habits and attitudes that have been successfully used over many years. To use the psychological jargon, 'extinctions' and 'reconditioning' may be necessary. Those managers who have successfully worked for many years in a stable environment, particularly with one company, can develop what has been called 'one repertoire of responses'. This means that when the situation changes they may work even harder at using trusted and tried methods to seek to regulate the problem even further, instead of using a set of new and more appropriate responses. This was demonstrated by some classic research, which also highlighted the need to have appropriate structures when dealing with rapid change.

193

One industry that has been particularly subjected to changes in its external environment over recent years is the financial services industry. The position may be shown thus:

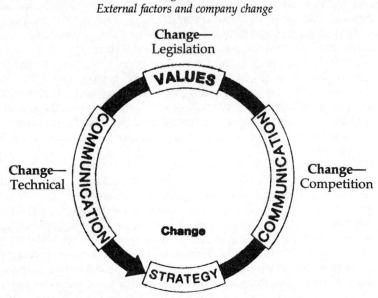

Figure 49
External factors and company change

Change—
Legislation

Change—
Technical

Change—
Competition

Change—
Market needs and social environment

(John Evans, 1984)

Change as a process
Organizational change is a process rather than an event. It takes time to recognize that a situation needs to be changed and further time to develop a plan to deal with it. In the end success depends upon new behaviour patterns and changes in working habits being adopted by those concerned. There are a number of distinguishing stages in the process.

Recognition of the need for change
This may be the most difficult of all stages. Ideally the need for change should be anticipated, otherwise events may develop to an extent where innovations have to be invented rapidly as a matter of crisis rather than in a planned, orderly manner. Yet
194

crucial in the acceptance of change is the rate of that change, since the more abrupt it is the more difficult acceptance may prove to be. One way to avoid this unhappy state is to make a point of regularly reviewing performance and operating methods.

It may be that a change is initiated as part of an overall company strategy, and not by the manager or supervisor of one of the departments involved. If this is so it does not mean that he has no role in the management of that change in his department: in fact he is likely to be concerned that the change is implemented as smoothly as possible. It is suggested that he checks with those responsible for the overall management of the change that all the factors about to be discussed have been taken into account, and that he draws up an action plan for his part of the management of the change in programme.

Analyse the situation
Here the socio-technical framework is a useful means of analysing how a change in one system, which may in isolation seem to be of little import, can have consequences for another of the systems. With the knowledge a manager has of her department and the people who work with her it should be possible to predict likely outcomes with reasonable accuracy. The socio-technical framework is particularly valuable for ensuring that the impact on the informal social system of changes in the other systems is not overlooked.

Make a plan of action
It is useful to think through and plan the various factors involved in the change and the methods to be used to manage them smoothly. The plan should not be too rigid; in most successful change programmes some modifications have to be made to cater for what is an inherently dynamic situation where all the factors and reactions are not precisely known. If the plan is not sufficiently flexible, these adjustments cannot be made and consequently the quality of the change suffers. The following factors should be considered when drawing up a plan.

Managing anxiety
Whether a change or innovation will be successful or not will depend to a major extent on those people directly concerned and the commitment they give to it. Securing such commitment, or at least a sufficient degree to enable the change to be successfully implemented, is not always easy. This is because of the understandable anxiety that people have about the way the change may affect them—their established working habits, aspirations, relationships

195

with others, career prospects etc. The *status quo* gives many people a security and familiarity which is comfortable and reassuring, and which is only to be willingly changed for a new situation whose benefits to them are manifest. One of the early but often unstated questions is 'how will this affect me?' An understanding of people's perception of a change and their reactions to it is clearly essential to its successful management, particularly so when an immediate reaction is one of resistance.

Figure 50
Change reaction check-list

Self	advancement possibilities	Work	amount
	salary		interest
	future		importance
	self image		challenge
	authority		work pressure
	influence		skill
	status		physical surroundings
			hours of work
Others	relationships with comrades, boss, subordinates, family		

Any experienced manager can recall many examples of resistance to change. Often the resistance is expressed in oblique ways and takes such forms as:

it is not necessary
it is being done too quickly
it is not being thought out
this is a step backwards; no-one asked us.

Some of these views may of course have validity for a particular situation but more frequently they reflect resistance to change.

To deal with the understandable anxiety about a change and the resistance to it that may be present it is necessary to be able to evaluate the change from the point of view of those concerned, not only in terms of the formal social system but also in terms of the informal one. The points in figure 50 above provide a useful checklist for summarizing the reactions of individuals or a group to a change. They are particularly useful in obtaining a sharper perspective on one or several causes of resistance that are likely to occur and which have to be managed. It also highlights the main perceived benefits that will accrue. In short it will enable a more accurate assessment of the situation to be made in order to work through a successful change of strategy.

There are two basic strategies which may be used to facilitate change; an attempt to increase acceptance or an attempt to reduce resistance as will be explored.

Force field analysis

This is a planning tool designed to help in identifying the forces present in a situation of change and in selecting an appropriate strategy. There are two types of forces: acceptance forces tending to initiate a change and resistance forces acting to restrain or decrease the acceptance forces. There exists a state of equilibrium when the sum of the strength of the acceptance forces equals the sum of the resistance forces.

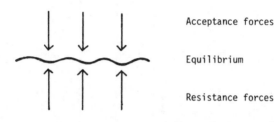

Acceptance forces

Equilibrium

Resistance forces

The equilibrium can be overcome by changing the balance between the forces in favour of the acceptance ones. If the acceptance forces are increased they often create even greater resistance so that the equilibrium is maintained. The preferred strategy then is to seek to reduce the restraining forces.

The following example will illustrate how such an analysis can be made so that the strength of the various forces is identified. Here a design engineer is being offered promotion to the post of engineering administrator in a different branch of the company some 120 miles away. Among the acceptance forces acting towards acceptance of the job are a salary increment, increase in status, new challenge etc. Those restraining forces acting against this include the social costs incurred, his enjoyment of his present type of work and the risks he perceives in the new situation. The strength of the various forces is as shown. It is likely here that an approach based on reducing the restraining forces such as through counselling, increasing his sense of security etc will then be more successful than increasing the acceptance forces.

These two sets of forces may be depicted in a diagram, with arrows representing the number and strength of the resistance and acceptance forces respectively as shown in the example in figure 51 overleaf.

The value of this kind of analysis is that a rigorous and planned approach is taken to what is so often done very casually. As situations may be changed by weakening the resistance forces or

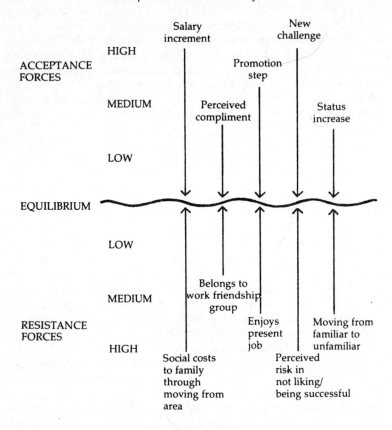

Figure 51
Acceptance versus resistance forces

strengthening the acceptance ones, each force identified should be considered in this light. Many change strategies only achieve limited success through encountering 'resistance to change'. Such resistance is often due to the natural and legitimate anxieties that people have about how the change might affect their working lives. It is not surprising that changes from established practices to new ways that can only be anticipated at the onset can arouse uneasiness or anxiety. Understanding the likely sources of anxiety will enable a manager to deal with it more readily. Generally too it is better to concentrate on reducing the resistance forces rather than on increasing the acceptance ones.

Roles and responsibilities

A major change is likely to demand some adjustment to roles and responsibilities. Quite naturally this can be a great concern to people, particularly as factors such as promotion paths, type of work performed, relationships with others and manning levels may be involved. These considerations require thought and planning.

A refinement of this will be seen in figure 52 overleaf. In the same way that with people a stimulus does not result directly in a response, but the response will come out of the experience, attitudes and background of the people it affects, then any initiation of change will have a perceived outcome depending upon such things as past experiences, personality, group influence, the degree of trust in the people concerned and the degree of participation in that change. As has been described, this is where corporate culture, or the expectations of how change is dealt with, is critically important. The evaluation of the outcome then depends very much on the perceived and often personalized outcome, and is likely to vary with different people. The evaluation can range from being destructive to beneficial, with corresponding reactions ranging again from opposition to active involvement. The aim of managing change effectively is to influence the perceived outcome of the people involved such that they are aware of the benefits and positive aspects of the intended change and that any negative aspects can be resolved. This requires a high degree of positive influencing skills on the part of the manager.

It is imperative that any issues about roles and responsibilities should be dealt with and communicated at an early stage in the change process. Even if no change in roles and responsibilities is envisaged it is worth communicating this, so that people know where they are and potential anxiety or high expectations can be allayed.

An examination of roles and responsibilities should also include a review of the reward system and training needs to equip people for a change in role.

Reward system

As the reward system will be of central interest to those concerned in the change, it is obviously important to consider the appropriateness and fairness of the system as it will apply in the new situation. Here it is not only the pay and salary structure that needs to be assessed but also factors such as promotion channels and the way tasks are structured in terms of the satisfaction, or otherwise, they provide. The total reward system and 'how it applies to me' is of particular concern to people when experiencing organizational change and communication must be especially clear and thorough when these points are introduced.

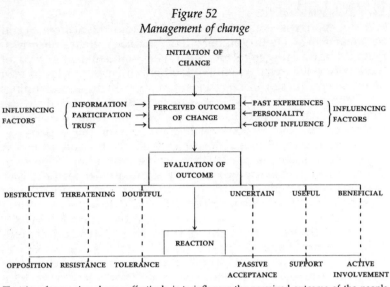

Figure 52
Management of change

The aim of managing change effectively is to influence the perceived outcome of the people involved such that they are aware of the benefits and positive aspects of the intended change and that any negative aspects can be resolved.

Source: David Hughes, 1986.

There are of course many systems of payment—measured day work, individual or group piece work, salary, merit payments and bonuses—and the appropriateness of these depends upon the particular situation. While it is beyond the scope of this chapter to discuss these in detail, the point must be made that it is crucial to take into account the fairness and equity of the payment system, as perceived by those affected by it. Money has a symbolic power which makes nonsense of the relatively small sum involved, as any personnel manager experienced in the administration of differentials would witness.

Training needs
It may be that a change programme is so acute that the need for training to equip people with additional skills is self-evident. When this is so the appropriate form of training can be introduced. But a 'grey area' sometimes occurs where, although there is to be some significant change in job content and skills, it is easy to assume that these will be rapidly acquired through experience. Although this might in fact be true, there is much merit in considering the—to him largely unknown—change in job content from the point of view of the person directly concerned. It is easy to assume that no training is necessary, yet such a viewpoint may reflect the greater
200

The reward system will be of central interest to those concerned in the change

knowledge and experience of the manager than what is actually felt by the person concerned. For example, if a person has been performing a job in a certain way for a number of years, a change to that established method of working, although relatively minor, may in anticipation at least assume such proportions that there is reluctance to depart from the known and the familiar. In such cases, and provided it is carried out sufficiently in advance, training has the added advantage of inducing reassurance and commitment as well as ensuring that the appropriate level of skill required for the new situation is developed.

Effective communication
This is crucial for the effective implementation of change. People must understand the reasons for change and be able to see the benefit it will bring in order for them to have sufficient commitment for the change to be successful. It is all too easy to assume that this will happen automatically: that is, because one is aware of the reasons and benefits they must also be apparent to all the other people involved. Yet frequently such an assumption is not a valid one.

Management style
People's support for a change can rarely be commanded. Rather it has to be elicited and without reasonable support the change is likely to be less than successful. An authoritarian style of communication is generally less conducive to gaining support than one that is more participative. The appropriate communication style to use obviously depends upon the situation and the nature of the change to be implemented. The choice of style and the methods and channels to be employed merit careful consideration. What can be said about participatory styles of communication is

that they have a greater potential for securing commitment, and often allow better quality decisions to be made. To be involved in the decision is more acceptable to many than having the decision thrust upon them. It also gives an opportunity for those concerned to ask questions about the change; such an opportunity results in further knowledge of what is involved and enables the manager to get feedback about how the change is being received. It also taps the knowledge that people have about the way things really work—part of the informal social system—and thus real difficulties and improvements can be discovered and acted upon. This of course requires that the plan be sufficiently flexible for modifications to be introduced.

It is perhaps appropriate to comment upon some observations made by those familiar with the Japanese approach to the management of organizational change. Typically before any major decision is taken, participation in the making of that decision is widely and deeply spread in the company. Many Western business men find that the negotiation of a contract with a Japanese firm appears to be an exasperatingly long affair, where often the same ground is covered many times with many different people. Once the contract is signed, however, its implementation is faster than many Western business men are used to and can cause some difficulties. The point is that under the Japanese system generally people are well acquainted with the nature of the change to be implemented, have participated widely in it, are familiar with what is expected of them and have worked through how it is to be implemented. This tends to contrast with the British system where relatively little time is spent making the decision, and much time taken in implementing it. Yet the implementation is frequently the most difficult part to manage smoothly. When all the difficulties inherent in change are considered this is not surprising. The management style and communication methods typically employed by many Japanese companies recognize this; they do much not only to affect the quality of the decision made but to ensure its smooth and rapid implementation.

Summary
One useful rule of thumb for deciding which communication approach is most appropriate comes through categorizing the decision in three main ways. The first type concerns decisions which need to be of high quality but involve a low acceptance threshold on the part of those concerned. Such decisons are those concerned with securing new orders: for example, as long as order books remain filled many workers do not feel strongly about having a say in such matters. The second type are those decisions that
202

require a high degree of acceptance from the people concerned but where the quality of decisions is not crucial from the manager's viewpoint, such as rotas etc. The third type are those issues which require both high quality and high acceptance: here a particularly high level of communication skill is required.

Activity plans
The text has indicated that the tendency is for change to occur in organizations at an accelerating rate. How the manager handles such change depends largely on his orientation to innovation generally, and his ability to think ahead and be flexible. One way to achieve this latter is to regard change as a process rather than an event, and thus to plan for it. The socio-technical framework provides a useful 'tool' to predict problems and guide the handling of a change, and field force analysis is a way of identifying and thinking through ways of overcoming resistance forces. The activity plan will enable you to know more about your own orientations to change and to test out 'thinking tools' in a variety of situations. In 1789 Ben Franklin wrote to a friend, 'But in this world nothing is certain but death and taxes'. He neglected to mention a third certainty . . . change.

Activity 1: Change orientations questionnaire
This questionnaire will allow you to examine your general orientation to change. The intent is more to help you think about, and examine your basic attitudes to change, rather than to provide a 'scientific' means of evaluating them. The results should therefore not be taken too seriously but do be honest with yourself when answering the questions.

Orientations questionnaire	Definitely yes	Generally yes	Mixed feelings	Generally no	Definitely no
1 Life today is much more pleasant than it was 10 years ago					
2 Decimalization has made shopping easier					
3 It is better to stick to what you know than to be trying new things you don't really know about					
4 It is only by altering the fundamental values of our society that real social progress can be made					
5 The risk in trying to change things is that they can turn out much worse					

203

Orientations questionnaire	Definitely yes	Generally yes	Mixed feelings	Generally no	Definitely no
6 I like to take my holidays at a place I have been before and know I will like					
7 Tradition is the brake on the progress of this country					
8 The 'realism' shown in some TV plays today is a major improvement					
9 I would be reluctant to move from where I now live					
10 My happiest days are yet to come					
11 Life is not perfect nowadays but it is much better than it used to be					
12 I prefer to eat in a place I know					
13 Change in dress fashion is a good thing					
14 Looking for new ways of doing things pays off more often than not					
15 Once I have arranged my office furniture the way I know it works, there is no point in trying to change it					
16 It pays to have a change of government once in a while					
17 A bird in the hand is worth two in the bush					
18 It is better to stay in a job that you know thoroughly and can do extremely well					
19 When I go out for a meal, I always try something I haven't eaten before					
20 Old friends are the best					
21 I feel slightly uncomfortable when I wear new clothes for the first time					
22 Have you introduced a major innovation at work in the last two years?					

Results key for questions nos 1, 2, 4, 7, 8, 10, 11, 13, 14, 16, 19, 22

Score	definitely yes	4
	generally yes	3
	mixed feelings	2
	generally no	1
	definitely no	0

for questions nos 3, 5, 6, 9, 12, 15, 17, 18, 20, 21

Score	definitely yes	0
	generally yes	1
	mixed feelings	2
	generally no	3
	definitely no	4

Add the scores for each question and enter on the continuum below

Change orientations

←Towards   Against→
_____
| | | | |
88   66   44   22   0

What can you infer from this?

Activity 2: predicting the consequences of change
Think of a situation such as:

A A change at work that you have experienced
B A residential course you have attended where you worked in a different way from what you do normally
C Your job in one company compared with a similar one elsewhere that you may have experienced
D You are required to plan the handling of a change from small offices to a large open-plan one.

Use the socio-technical model to trace through the changes, or likely consequences, of changes in one system and their influences and impact on the others. In doing this list at least two of the changes in each of the systems that collectively comprise the total socio-technical system.

Activity 3: identifying and overcoming resistance forces
Choose one of the following:

A You want to persuade your wife/husband to spend your annual holiday abroad instead of visiting his/her parents
B You have been offered a promotion but it means living in a different town 200 miles away
C A work situation you wish to change.

Using a change reaction force field diagram, identify the nature and strength of the various resistance forces and acceptance forces; using this as a basis, sketch out a strategy to cope with the problem.

Activity 4: how equipped are you for future change?
One of the ironies about future change is that it cannot be predicted with any certainty. Nevertheless, as with planning generally, a degree of planning will be most valuable. In the same way that an aircraft's flight plan can be modified when different circumstances

205

prevail in flight, then a plan will at least give the basis on which actions can be modified. Also certain characteristics for coping with rapid change are being widely predicted, as is the way organizations will need to cope with such change. The following checklist is not scientific, or totally inclusive; it attempts simply to allow you to 'stocktake' some of the factors involved, at a personal, organizational and wider environment level.

Personal transitions management and life planning
1 Have you taken clear *personal* responsibility for your career?
2 Do you understand change and the change process?
3 Do you understand yourself and your personal make-up well?

Skills for change
1 Can you 'vision' exciting possibilities in the future?
2 Can you translate strategy into practice?
3 Are your team management skills high?
4 Do you have the courage needed not to stop short?
5 Is your personal power and influence sufficient to bargain for the resources necessary?
6 Do you have skills in finding and using information and resources?

Change mastership
1 Can you promote organizational cultures?
2 Can you generate organizational cultures that promote change?
3 Can you do what needs to be done rather than just do your job in the sense of obeying the rules?
4 Is change an opportunity for you in the sense of providing exhilaration, challenge, the option to exercise choice and to be a 'renaissance' person?
5 Do you feel secure in flexible situations when you are not in complete control?

Victims of change
1 Do you see change as an enemy?
2 Are you fearful of it?
3 Will it involve loss of control and security that comes from control?

Career
1 Can you work well on the edge of your competence?
2 Would you prefer to have wide multi-disciplinary experience or stay within the one area of expertise?
3 Do you view having a multi-career and changing work/life as threatening?

206

Problem solving
Is your problem-solving approach based on an insightful, integrative approach as well as rationality and logic?

Organization skills
1 Can you work well in an adhocracy with fluid, non-hierarchical structures?
2 How do you feel about a significant part of your working life being in short-term task forces that achieve and disband?
3 How well do you cope with planning?
4 How do decentralized, less tidy structures appeal?
5 Can you communicate well both horizontally and informally, as opposed to vertically and formally?
6 Can you communicate enough to get the job done well but so that the system isn't overloaded?

Monitoring the environment
1 How well can you self-manage your job?
2 How good is your boundary spanning within your job?
3 Do you prefer to be rewarded on performance or other factors?
4 Can you answer clearly the question of 'What business are we in?'
5 Can you clearly identify the consequences of demographic shift in your business?
6 Can you state what economic, social and governmental regulatory changes will occur in your industry over the next five years?
7 How precisely can you describe and monitor your organization's culture?

Towards a post-industrial society
How comfortable are you with
    new technology?
    less distinction between management and workers?
    much more fluid markets?
    more women and two-wage families in the workforce?
    no lifetime employment?
    much greater education?

13 Motivation: why people work well

This chapter is about managing motivation. It focuses both upon our understanding of individuals and ourselves in relation to important aspects of job situations. Motivation is defined in terms of performance and is placed in the perspective of trends in work and society. Two activity plans are integrated with the text.

Motivation: what is it?

To understand motivation at work it is necessary to examine factors affecting an individual's performance, which will be between two limits. The upper limit is the highest level that can be achieved, given the individual's abilities and the technical system within which he is working. The lower limit is the level which management is prepared to tolerate. It is not difficult to imagine that the distance between the upper and lower limits can be very wide. Where an individual's performance actually is between these limits depends upon his motivation, or will to work well.

Figure 53 opposite suggests that there are four ways in which a manager may influence his subordinate's performance.

Improving the technical system
Improvements in such things as technology, methods, procedures, equipment, information systems or controls can be seen as improvements in the technical system. The effect this has is to raise the upper limit of performance that can be achieved, although this in itself does not guarantee that improvements will occur.

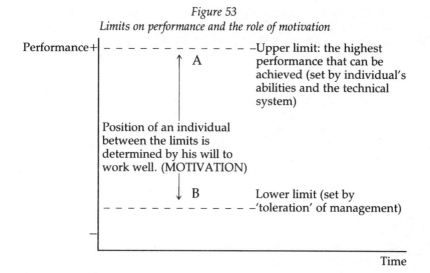

Figure 53
Limits on performance and the role of motivation

Performance +
Upper limit: the highest performance that can be achieved (set by individual's abilities and the technical system)

A

Position of an individual between the limits is determined by his will to work well. (MOTIVATION)

B

Lower limit (set by 'toleration' of management)

Time

Developing abilities
If abilities are developed, perhaps by training, guiding, coaching and appraisal, then again the upper limit will have been raised.

Raising the toleration level
The toleration level is usually ill defined, and unilateral attempts to raise it by work study, threats or getting tough is usually a rapid means of teaching a manager that he is not the only source of power and influence in his part of the organization.

Positively influencing motivation
An individual in position A will be highly motivated; in position B he will be totally unmotivated or 'alienated' from his work. An increase in motivation will have the effect of moving performance in the direction of A.

If performance is dependent in part upon 'the will to perform', what the individual wants (personal goals), and the degree to which task performance is seen as the pathway to achieving such goals, are important matters for the manager of people.

Activity plan 1: what motivates you?
As a means of understanding the realities of motivation, and in preparation for the text which follows, it is suggested that you undertake the following activity.

Think of a work (or study) situation which has produced very high motivation for you, so that you are near position A in figure 53. It will be a situation in which you had good feelings about the work and which led to a high willingness to work well.

Choose another situation which has had the opposite effect of bad feelings and low motivation, so that you were near position B in figure 53.

In turn, think closely about both these situations. Describe to yourself (or a colleague, if you are able to share this with another) the two cases you have chosen.

Analyse both cases. Can you identify six factors crucial to the high motivation and another six which were associated with the low motivation? See if you can boil these down to one word or phrase each. Do you think these factors are exclusive to you, or do they apply to many people and situations?

Motivation: is there a problem?

Observers of society and work organizations have identified many trends within industrial society which have had the effect of lowering the will to work well. During the twentieth century in developed societies our educational and often political institutions have encouraged the individual to think creatively and independently, to acquire skills and foster talent, and to seek involvement, influence and identity in the community. At the same time, developments in the world of work have often run counter to these growing aspirations and expectations, as figure 54 opposite suggests. To the extent that there is truth in this analysis, motivation at work has become progressively more difficult, and it is a task of management to help put back the stimulus at work which organizational trends have removed. Success will not only increase performance but equally important will also remove a great deal of frustration and apathy at work.

The motivation problem in figure 54 is that an increasing 'division of labour' is a characteristic of the development of many organizations. This is taken to mean that there is an increase in role specialization, with individuals doing more and more of less and less; that there is greater difference between groups and levels in terms of job type, status, rewards, power, influence and so on; that systems and technology become more complex; and that there is an increase in the scale of the organization. Associated with this trend are factors which reduce motivation and increase alienation. For example, it is suggested that people feel increasingly powerless to influence what happens to them at work. The tasks which are performed become meaningless; it is more difficult to see the relevance or outcome of what you do. Individuals feel more isolated and groups notice differences rather than what they have in
210

Figure 54
Perspective and trends: motivation

	− division of labour +	
	(Specialization : differentiation : complexity : size)	
influence	control over work and environment	powerless
meaning	task performed	meaningless
integrated	anomie: identity and common standards	isolated
intrinsic satisfaction	work	means to an end
motivation		alienation
stimulus from job situation	+ −	

common. This is referred to as anomie and is a state of norm-lessness; lack of consensus upon basic standards; and a lack of feeling of roots or belonging. In addition, the satisfactions from doing a job well are lost and work is only seen as a means to an end, such as improving material rewards.

All this means that the stimulus to work well is removed progressively from the job situation, the individual's alienation becomes more acute and the manager's problem of motivating staff is increasingly severe.

What can the manager do to motivate?
The answers to this fundamental question lie in two areas.

Understanding individuals
What makes an individual tick, in terms of work motivation? What is there within a human being which affects behaviour and performance?

Situational factors
Secondly, what are the key situational factors which stimulate the will to work well, and what approaches might be made to make sure they are present?

Managing motivation: understanding individuals

If an organization or a manager attempts to motivate people, the action taken will depend to a considerable extent on the assumptions made about the nature of man. Throughout history a number of assumptions have been made. Over the last 60 years or so managers, sociologists, psychologists and economists have had three main streams of thought about the nature of man, his needs and thus what motivates him. The views are still prevalent today in that many organizations base their motivation strategies around one of them. The three sets of assumptions are called

rational—economic man
social man
self actualizing man.

These were described in chapter 3, where it was suggested that complex man would be a more useful concept.

If the view of 'complex man' is accepted, it can be seen that different strategies are appropriate to particular people at different times. This implies the importance of sensitivity in diagnosing differing needs. The snowflake analogy will illustrate this point: all snowflakes share the same overall characteristics, but when examined under a microscope the crystalline structure of each is found to be uniquely different.

The acceptance of man as complex is an important step forward for the manager who may oversimplify, make wrong assumptions, or have fixed stereotyped views about people at work. It is still necessary to get to grips with the complexity and Maslow's need hierarchy, also discussed in chapter 3, is a useful thinking tool for this purpose.

Managing motivation: situational strategies

The dual factor theory

It has been indicated that there are two key elements to understanding an individual's motivation to work well. One is the individual and the other is the total situation in which the individual is working.

A framework that can provide useful insights into the links between individual and situational factors is that of Herzberg's dual factor theory. He obtained descriptions of work events which had given rise to good or bad feelings, and then identified the key factors in each event. When the factors were collated, some were mainly linked to 'bad' feelings and others mainly to 'good' ones. This gave rise to the dual factor theory, involving maintenance (or hygiene) factors and motivator factors (*see* figure 55 on page 214).

Maintenance factors
If these are seen as adequate, or if they are improved, they have no effect upon performance through the 'will to work'. They tend to be taken for granted after a short time. The impact upon feelings is neutral (1) (*see* figure 55).

If they are seen as 'inadequate' or 'deteriorating', they cause dissatisfaction and may lower performance by having a negative effect on the 'will to work'. Hence their function is to 'maintain' an existing performance level rather than to improve it through motivation, but they are important for attracting/repelling or keeping/losing staff. They 'get' and help 'keep' but don't in themselves stimulate motivation to work well (2).

Motivator factors
These factors give rise to good feelings and raise performance by influencing the 'will to work well'. They have a variable impact and duration (3).

A summary of Herzberg's findings is shown in figure 56 on page 215 but you may wish to complete the activity plan before making reference to it.

Activity plan 2: situational factors and motivation
Below are six situational factors. Assess each one in terms of the degree and duration of its positive impact upon the will to work well and performance (refer to figure 55 overleaf). Identify the conditions which need to apply to individuals and situations for a factor to be effective as a motivator, rather than a maintenance/hygiene factor.

1 Promotion and prospects of promotion
2 Money: financial incentives
3 Competition: both between individuals and groups
4 Working conditions: physical; amenities; fringe benefits
5 Management style: patterns of behaviour towards others
6 Job satisfaction: stimulus from the job itself

Promotion and prospects of promotion
Promotion
The achievement of promotion and the new job could provide a stimulus to the will to work well. The effect might be very similar to job enrichment. In some circumstances, for some people, this could last for a substantial time. When the 'challenge' wears off, the prospects of further promotion may continue to have an influence.

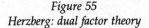

Figure 55
Herzberg: dual factor theory

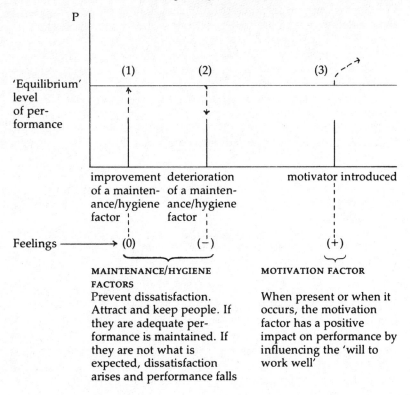

	MAINTENANCE/HYGIENE FACTORS	MOTIVATION FACTOR
	Prevent dissatisfaction. Attract and keep people. If they are adequate performance is maintained. If they are not what is expected, dissatisfaction arises and performance falls	When present or when it occurs, the motivation factor has a positive impact on performance by influencing the 'will to work well'

Prospects—opportunities

Some managers attempt to stimulate performance by making their subordinates aware that future advancement depends *in part* upon current attitudes and performance. To have an impact, one condition necessary is that the subordinates feel that the opportunities really exist and are attainable (ie there is a fair chance of GETTING promotion).

McClelland's work on achievement motivation indicates that there will be no stimulus if the odds are on getting promotion (eg if a subordinate knows that the criterion is mainly seniority, and all he has to do is to sit tight). On the other hand, if the odds are heavily against getting promotion (eg 50 people competing for one opening) subordinates are unlikely to be stimulated because the chances are 'unrealistic'.

Some organizations are now actively developing alternative career

214

Figure 56
Motivators and maintenance factors

MAINTENANCE		FACTOR	MOTIVATOR		
IMPACT DURATION	FREQUENCY MENTIONED		FREQUENCY MENTIONED	IMPACT DURATION	
short	medium	achievement	very high	medium short	more likely to be a *motivator*: the most frequently mentioned
long	medium	recognition	very high	medium short	more likely to be a *motivator*
long	medium	work itself	high	long	more likely to be a *motivator*: long lasting
medium	low	responsibility	very high	long	more likely to be a *motivator*: the longest lasting
medium	low	advancement	medium	long	more likely to be a *motivator*: long lasting
medium	very high	company policy and administration	very low	long	more likely to be *maintenance*: most frequently mentioned cause of dissatisfaction
short	high	superior's technical competence	low	long	more likely to be *maintenance*, but can motivate long term
short	medium	relations with superior	low	long	more likely to be *maintenance*, but can motivate long term
short	medium	working conditions	very low	short	more likely to be *maintenance*
long	low	salary	low	medium short	equal *motivator* and *maintenance* frequency, but bad feelings last longer than good
medium	low	personal growth	low	long	long lasting when mentioned as *motivator*
medium long	very low	security	very low	medium	not often mentioned, but significant duration when it is

Summary of the findings of F Herzberg *et al* in 12 studies covering 1,685 people in varying jobs and levels.

routes for staff, so that there are fewer 'single ladder' dead man's shoes situations. Where no prospects exist, this can lead to substantial dissatisfaction from those who want promotion, and often gives rise to mild dissatisfaction amongst many who profess *not* to want it.

Prospects—management's supporting activities
In order to achieve effective promotions, and to maximize the opportunities for the motivational stimulus of people in their current positions, management should attempt to meet a number of conditions:

(a) the criteria for promotion should be apparent
(b) the managers selecting for promotion should try to be seen to be 'fair'
(c) effective appraisal (formal and/or informal) should be conducted so that more accurate assessments can be made about subordinates' potential
(d) staff with potential should receive appropriate training, coaching, counselling and development
(e) dangers of using promotion prospects as a motivational tactic should be avoided (eg raising 'false' hopes, by appearing to make 'promises'; 'overselling' prospects).

Prospects—are people interested?
An individual must be in the position of WANTING promotion if the 'prospects' are to provide motivation. This depends upon how that individual perceives the balance between the rewards/punishments associated with promotion. Many factors seem to be taken into account, and could include comparing the current job and the 'promotion' job in terms of satisfaction of social needs; job satisfaction; responsibilities; security/anxiety; financial rewards; geographic mobility and location; power and status.

If there are real opportunities, based on merit; if the individual aspires towards promotion; and if management provides the 'supporting' conditions, then promotion prospects will be an effective motivational stimulus.

Money: financial incentives
Most people have to work to earn money in order to live. Their choice of job and decision to stay or leave is influenced by money, amongst other things. However, as far as motivation and performance is concerned, the question is whether money can be used to stimulate the will to work well, once the individual has been attracted and is being kept.

It has become fashionable to discount to some degree money as a motivator. Many practising managers still rate money as significant as an influence on the will to work well, although there is a recognition that other factors have much potency. The problem is that motivational strategies based on money also bring with them a number of negative effects. Also, the greater the immediacy of the financial incentive in terms of its control by individuals and the speed of the reward, the greater its motivational effect, but equally the greater is its potential for unintended and negative consequences. When evaluating a scheme it is important to distinguish between its intended consequences, such as its impact upon individual performance, and its unintended consequences such as its negative impact upon other factors necessary for the achievement of organizational objectives. Even when conditions are present which permit a 'successful' scheme, the cost may be high. It is for these reasons that we will point out some of the typical difficulties of various incentive schemes, as well as their advantages.

Incentive schemes recognize that people quickly get used to a wage/salary level and come to expect it as of right. After a large salary increase a person may make a conscious effort for better performance, but typically soon comes to see that salary level as his due and the stimulus wears off. Regular increments too do not seem to motivate people other than by causing them to stay in the organization. This is not to say that the 'effort reward' bargain between the employee and the organization does not need to be perceived as fair and equitable by the employee. If employees are receiving a base rate or salary which they regard as unjust for the work they are required to perform, this is bound to affect their level of motivation.

Wage/effort incentives
The common feature of such schemes is that they are based on measurement and the money reward is directly related to 'measured' performance. Such schemes include payment by results, piece rates, bonus schemes, commission etc and may be based on the individual or a group.

The attraction of schemes based upon the individual is, as we have stated, the greater immediacy of the reward and its direct motivational effect; equally, the greater are the problems associated with it. We will first examine schemes based on individuals.

(i) *conditions necessary for an effective scheme*
(a) The individual's dominant need is to maximize his earnings.
(b) Within work the positive forces associated with the need for money are sufficient to overcome opposing forces and lead

to greater effort. These opposing forces may result from:

fears of rate cutting or working oneself out of a job

a reluctance or inability to work harder. This may result from boredom, fatigue, self-set and fixed earning targets

a determination of the individual to control his own pace and effort, and the preference for elbow-room rather than an extra pound

group enforced standards of performance; which preserve the social system of the group, and are lower than management standards

(c) The scheme must be intelligible, so that the individual can clearly relate effort to earnings.

(d) The job should be standardized and repetitive, with a short time cycle and a minute breakdown of operations, requiring mainly physical effort and little discretion. (Craft, non-production and process jobs may be inappropriate.)

(e) The individual must be able to control his results and pace.

(f) The individual is not a member of a cohesive task-interest group.

(g) There is a fund of goodwill between management and employees prior to the introduction of the scheme.

(ii) *unintended consequences of wage-effort incentives*

(a) Increase in the sources of conflict.

(b) Creativity directed to beating the system.

(c) Resistance to change and inflexibility.

(d) Loss of control: management to worker; union official to shop steward.

(e) Administrative costs.

The effectiveness of individual incentive schemes becomes limited when large numbers of people are performing identical tasks, so that an individual by superior performance can threaten the rewards and security of the majority. It follows that individual rewards are difficult to apply effectively when a number of people are doing the same work and sharing the same fate in mass production organizations. This is one reason why schemes based upon the group have become prevalent. Another is the fact that in large scale organizations the work of any one man is highly dependent upon what his colleagues are doing. That is, tasks are interdependent. Group incentives then become logical.

Measured day work is to some degree an extension of this and is an attempt to iron out some of the difficulties associated with individual variations in performance. The essence of this is that each worker contracts to perform at an agreed, measured rate, in return for a fixed incentive payment. Such schemes lend themselves most readily to mass production systems where the work performed is relatively simple. Another approach is to rely on different rates for groups within a total group, so that promotion or upgrading becomes the most potent type of reward. Here the employee is rewarded by being moved to a different category of workers on a higher pay scale. This is often perceived as being more equitable than differential rewards within the same sub-group. The difficulty is that such promotion is often based on factors such as seniority, attendance and the observance of rules rather than on individual performance on the job.

Quality development incentives
The common feature of this type of scheme is that a periodic assessment is made of the 'improvement' of an individual over a range of job related factors such as time keeping, skills, flexibility and cooperation (eg merit rating).

(i) *advantages*
(a) It provides a relatively stable addition to the basic rate.
(b) A number of job qualities are taken into account and not just effort.

(ii) *problems*
(a) The felt fairness of the assessment and administration.
(b) There is often union resistance, as it can be seen to be an interference with collective bargaining.
(c) There is a substantial time gap between assessments.
(d) It can promote conflict between individuals or groups.

Participation, commitment or flexibility incentives
There are a number of approaches. As well as the particular disadvantages and problems associated with each, they share some common limitations, such as:

the remoteness of the reward from individual performance.
the perceived arbitrary determination of the size of the bonus.

The 'Scanlon' Plan
This is a factory or 'unit' wide group bonus scheme based on the ratio of total manpower costs to total sales value of output during a period, usually four weeks. An important part of the scheme is that it is administered by a committee drawn from all levels of employees.

(i) *advantages*
(a) It is concerned not just with output but with cost reduction.

(b) Acceptance and adjustment to change is rewarded.
(c) Teamwork and cooperation are encouraged.
(d) It recognizes the social needs to participate and to be involved in the endeavour of the group.
(e) Creativity can be rewarded.
(f) It provides a structure for worker (or union) and management cooperation.

(ii) problems
(a) The readjustment of bonus proportions may be resisted by employees when capital investment has changed the situation.
(b) It is difficult to relate efforts to rewards.
(c) The bonus may be affected by factors outside of worker's control, which requires that employees share all the organization's risks.

Profit sharing
Here the aims are similar to those of the Scanlon Plan, but there is no committee machinery for cooperation and creativity.

(i) advantages
(a) It can create a sense of citizenship and partnership with the organization.
(b) It is relatively simple to administer.

(ii) problems
(a) The rewards may seem remote.
(b) If the rewards are variable this may be resented, while a fixed reward may have no incentive effect.

Productivity bargaining
This is a negotiated agreement aimed at reducing unit costs, which involves employers buying out 'restrictive' or 'protective' practices to permit more efficient manpower utilization by redeployment or increased labour flexibility. If unit costs are reduced by reorganizing work, some of the savings are given to employees for cooperating in cost reduction. Thus it is not strictly a motivational strategy in the sense that it is a direct incentive to work well; it is rather an inducement to adopt more efficient work practices. However, a by-product may be motivation by job enlargement. There are a number of prerequisites before productivity bargaining can be successfully entered into, and these include:

real scope for improving work practices

mutual trust based on a history of fair and open dealing with
the union

employees to be open to the idea that the deal can be in their
collective interests.

(i) *advantages*
(a) Gains can be high.
(b) It can promote more productive attitudes.

(ii) *problems*
(a) It can be extremely time consuming in its negotiation, requiring
the fullest possible management/union consultation.
(b) Resistance, often based upon fears of skill devaluation and
redundancy, needs to be overcome.
(c) Although the reward to the organization may be high, the
initial cost is also high.
(d) Once a price has been paid for a 'restrictive' practice, it may
encourage the periodic development of new practices.

Competition: both between individuals and groups

Types of competition

Competition may be instigated by employees themselves, or may
be induced by management explicitly by schemes such as league
tables and awards, or implicitly by differential recognition given
to individuals and groups. It may be at the level of the individual
competing with himself; individuals competing with individuals;
or groups with groups.

Competition is based upon performance feedback, and this
element of knowing how well you are doing seems to be important
for motivation. The 'Maslow' needs of reputation, self esteem and
perhaps self fulfilment appear to be the moving forces.

Individuals often set themselves targets or deadlines and get
satisfaction from achieving them. Jointly established targets may
have a similar result, although the impact seems to be reduced the
less influence the individual has. Imposed targets, in this sense,
would be the least motivating.

Competition between individuals can take the form of open
performance comparison. For example, identifying the best pro-
ducers, top salesmen or best time-keepers.

Inter-group competition may be between groups on the same
location, on different sites doing similar jobs or even in different
divisions of an organization. It could be by the periodic publication
of performance league tables or simply by spreading such information on the grapevine.

The rewards of winning may be tangible or intangible. Cash

221

prizes or gifts in kind are common, particularly amongst salesmen. Other methods are different coloured uniforms or badges for the best performers, praise, or simply the pleasure of winning.

Problems
Competition is often problematic because:

(a) It can be seen as management manipulation.
(b) It can threaten work quality standards.
(c) It may be regarded as unfair, with the dice loaded against some individuals or groups.
(d) It may encourage conflict, which could be counterproductive. For example, in one case a company stimulated competition between shifts. When a particular shift began to win every time, investigation showed that its members were sabotaging the shift which followed them, sometimes by not completing 'handover' tasks or by causing minor equipment break-downs.
(e) It may lead to anxiety if the rewards are wanted too badly. Mental and physical performance can suffer if people try too hard. This is similar to the effect which Herzberg attributed to most carrot or stick motivation approaches, such as the inducement of fear by threats. He called these KITA factors, which politely translates to kick in the pants.

Conditions for effectiveness
Competition is likely to be more effective when

(a) There is an individualistic rather than group orientation to work.
(b) Collaboration is not required between the competitors.
(c) Ego needs are active.
(d) Competitors feel there is an equal chance of winning.
(e) The rewards are valued.
(f) The scheme has novelty value.
(g) It is felt to be fair.

Working conditions: physical; amenities; fringe benefits
There are a number of components of working conditions—the work environment in which people operate. It is useful to categorize these so that elements that have motivational implications may be identified.

The physical environment
(a) Space, light, heat, decor.

(b) Workplace layout.
(c) Danger, dirt, noise, hygiene.

Ergonomic conditions
(a) The relationship between people and machines/equipment, so that equipment is designed as a person-machine, rather than just a machine system.

Amenity provisions
(a) Refreshment, breaks, catering, luncheon vouchers, facilities for shift workers.
(b) Toilets, washrooms, showers, baths.
(c) Cloakrooms, drying rooms, personal lockers.
(d) Recreation, rest-rooms, gardens, sports and social club.

Fringe benefits
(a) Pension schemes.
(b) Payment during illness.
(c) Holiday entitlement.
(d) Working hours and 'flexitime'.
(e) Company car, home, share options.
(f) Travel concession.
(g) Medicare, dentistry, chiropody, physiotherapy etc.

Figure 57
The links between working conditions and performance

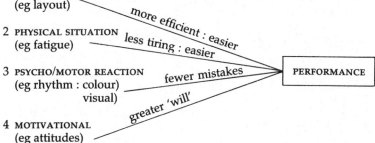

Some aspects of working conditions have a critical impact upon performance, but as figure 57 indicates, these are not necessarily due to increased motivation. It is probable that working conditions are primarily maintenance/hygiene factors and that improvement in them will have at best a short term impact upon the will to work well. The improvement will soon become part of an individual or group's expectations and taken for granted. If they deteriorate, it

223

is likely that performance will decline as bad feelings increase. This is the 'maintenance' factor effect.

Indirect motivational impact of working conditions
(a) *Physical/technical change* may affect task relationships and physical proximity, which in turn may affect social relationships and job attitudes.
(b) *Status symbols* may be attributed to different levels of working conditions, such as office and carpet size; type of company car; or the key to the executive lavatory. These are important to some individuals, and the desire to gain these symbols may be highly motivating.
(c) *Job satisfaction* may be provided by improved working conditions, which make it possible to do a better job.
(d) *Concern for people* may be demonstrated by interest and improvements in working conditions, and this in itself could affect attitudes to work and the will to perform well.

Management style: patterns of behaviour towards others
Management style was described in the chapter with that title as the pattern of behaviour that a manager uses in his relationships with others, particularly subordinates. Three dimensions were identified (*see* figure 58 opposite).

Research evidence and experience suggest that management style can be potent, both as a motivator and maintenance factor. It needs to be emphasized that it is not always one style mode which works as a motivator; the impact of style depends very much on the situation in which it is exercised.

Commentary on figure 58
It does seem that consistent exercise of a style at the extreme left hand position is likely to produce dissatisfaction, or at least have a neutral impact on the will to work well.

Style (a) can be motivating at any point on the scale, but it is probably longer lasting and has greater impact as the behaviour moves towards the right, until it approaches the abdication position. Part of the explanation may be that a 'directive' style constrains or forces performance, which will revert when the source of constraint is removed; for example, when the boss is away. Many people find that the trust displayed together with the involvement and ownership feelings element of a participant style lead to 'instrinsic' rather than 'extrinsic' motivation. That is to say, individuals are more likely to be self motivated.
Style (b) depends upon individual needs and expectations. For
224

Figure 58
Three dimensions of management style

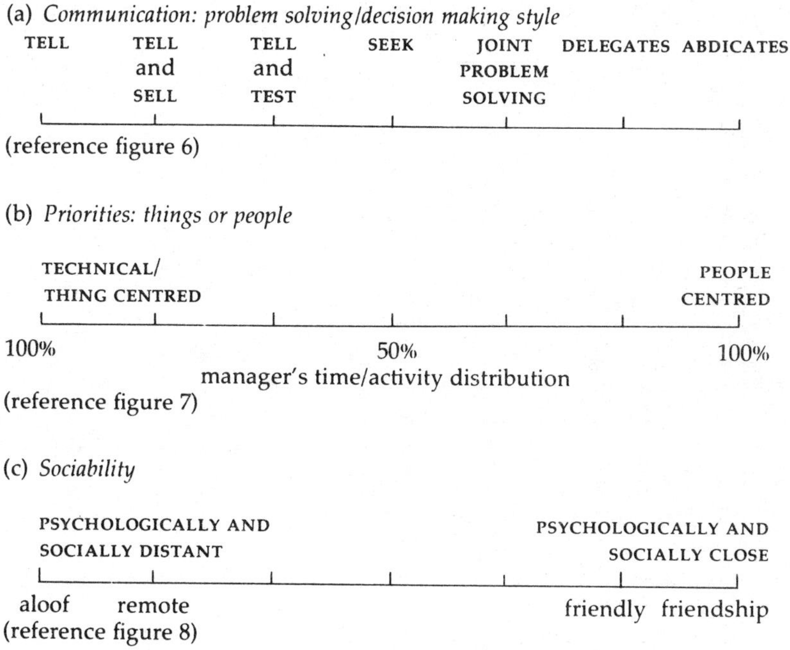

(a) *Communication: problem solving/decision making style*

TELL	TELL and SELL	TELL and TEST	SEEK	JOINT PROBLEM SOLVING	DELEGATES	ABDICATES

(reference figure 6)

(b) *Priorities: things or people*

TECHNICAL/ THING CENTRED						PEOPLE CENTRED

100% 50% 100%

manager's time/activity distribution

(reference figure 7)

(c) *Sociability*

PSYCHOLOGICALLY AND SOCIALLY DISTANT				PSYCHOLOGICALLY AND SOCIALLY CLOSE

aloof   remote   friendly friendship

(reference figure 8)

example, the subordinate who is dedicated to the technical aspects of his task will respond to the technical centred boss. Others will respond to the concern demonstrated for their personal needs. The people centred style, by definition, identifies frustrations which result in dissatisfaction and, to the extent that it assists in their removal, will be a maintenance factor.

Style (c) once again depends upon the subordinates' expectations related to their need for psychological space. An aloof boss, who makes no social demands upon subordinates may fit the subordinate who wants to be alone. Relationships which are felt to be bad can be a dissatisfier, and a degree of sociability will often prevent this.

There are a number of style characteristics associated with work behaviour and attitudes that frequently occur in management research findings. The following are often linked with good feelings and positive job attitudes:

keeping subordinates informed of policy, plans and expectation
giving feedback upon performance

225

giving praise and recognition
hearing complaints, grievances and problems.

It is wiser to talk about probabilities rather than certainties when assessing the effect of a single factor such as a particular mode of management style. Nevertheless, management style does appear to have a substantial impact upon feelings, motivation and performance.

Job satisfaction: stimulus from the job itself

The relationship between the individual and his job tasks and responsibilities is seen by many as the vital motivation factor. In recent years many efforts have been made by managers and organizations to systematically harness motivation through job satisfaction. These approaches have various labels, such as job enrichment, job enlargement, job design, work reform, work restructuring and democratization of work. The essence of this approach is the relationship between the size of the job, the size of the individual and his potential for growth.

(1)

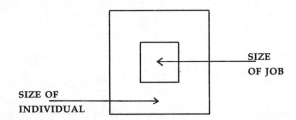

The individual's abilities and skills are greater than the demands made upon him by the size of the tasks or duties that he performs in the job. In these circumstances there will be no stimulus to work well from the job itself and the work will only be performed for other reasons, such as money, status or social rewards.

(2)

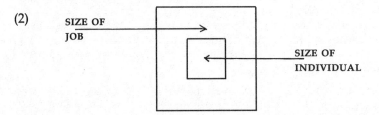

The individual's *current* abilities and skills are less than the opportunities for using them that exist within the tasks or duties that he could perform in the job. If he has the aspiration, potential and support to develop, the process of growth and the acquisition

226

and use of greater skills/abilities will provide stimulus to work well, at the same time as providing personal satisfaction.

The job size includes:

(a) Time cycle of tasks; from start to finish, before repeating the task.
(b) Range of tasks, which make up an individual's job.
(c) Responsibility, autonomy, judgement, decision making scope.

An increase in any single factor is an increase in the size of a job.

Criteria for 'good' job design
Over recent years much has become known about the factors which are important in 'good' job design. By 'good' is meant the design of a job so that taken into account are both the psychological requirements that people have of their work, and the requirements of the organization for effective performance, commitment and involvement. It may be said that sufficient is now known about job design for the principles involved to be no longer at the stage of academic debate, but rather for it to have become an established technology. Certainly there is remarkable common ground in the criteria identified by the various researchers.

(a) Optimum variety of tasks within the job.
(b) A meaningful pattern of tasks which gives to each job a semblance of a single overall task.
(c) Optimum length of work cycle.
(d) Some scope for setting standards of quantity and quality of production and a suitable feedback of knowledge of results.
(e) The inclusion in the job of some of the auxiliary and preparatory tasks.
(f) The tasks included in the job should include some degree of care, skill, knowledge, or effort that is worthy of respect in the community.
(g) The job should make some perceivable contribution to the utility of the product for the consumer.
(h) Adequate 'elbow room' in the sense that people feel, to a reasonable degree, that they are their own bosses. This involves worker discussion and decision making, account-ability and responsibility.
(i) Opportunities for learning on the job and going on learning. This provides stimulating motivation but requires adequate feedback of results and also goal setting at an appropriate level.
(j) The satisfying use of valued skills and abilities.
(k) The optimal level of variety and interest to suit personal tolerance levels.

(l)   Mutual support and respect, sometimes called social interaction, ie conditions where they can and do get willing help from their workmates.

(m) Meaningful and worthwhile work, including a perceived contribution to product utility, ie a sense of purpose.

(n)   A desirable future not necessarily implying promotion.

It has also become obvious that, in the eyes of the worker, some of these requirements are more important than others. For example, while people may become habituated to a lack of variety, they rarely become so to a lack of adequate 'elbow room'. It has also been shown that their relative importance varies from time to time depending on the workers' circumstances.

Approaches to harnessing motivation through job satisfaction
Unfortunately there is no single and simple way of constructing an 'ideal' job which not only caters for the needs of the organization but to a large measure for the psychological needs of individuals. One problem is that there are too many variables. People display tremendous variations in their abilities and preferences: in fact even a single individual's skills, knowledge and ambitions vary widely over a period of time. Technology, production, jobs and many other circumstances interrelate in complicated ways and are constantly changing. It is therefore hopeless to look for any generally applicable balance between all factors: a solution that will fit all situations. A 'right' solution can only be valid in the circumstances for which it is formulated and depends upon a careful diagnosis of that situation.

Nevertheless a number of approaches to work restructuring have evolved which provide a useful framework for considering approaches that may be taken. Each will be briefly described in turn.

Job rotation
An arrangement whereby operators are encouraged to alternate around differing work stations in an attempt to relieve monotony and increase variety. The component tasks themselves are not enlarged or enriched. The rotation is usually at the decision of a supervisor rather than being decided by the working group. The classic example is from the electronics industry where, instead of spending the whole day soldering in one type of transistor, an operator will move from station to station during the day to perform, at separate times, a number of functions.

Job enlargement
This usually implies the process of broadening one person's job
228

by bringing into it a set of tasks previously performed by several other individuals. This is 'horizontal' enlargement, ie the additional tasks do not necessarily require increased skills or responsibility, but simply make a more meaningful whole. The classic example, again from the electronics industry, is where instead of assembling one component into a sub-assembly, operators assemble the complete sub-assembly as a whole. It is important to note that most successful forms of work restructuring based on the individual have meant enlarging jobs both horizontally and vertically.

Job enrichment
This usually necessitates the restructuring of an individual job so that it is extended vertically; responsibilities previously located higher up the line of command are brought into the enriched job. A simple example is the machinist who is taught to service his own machine, or the process operator who is made responsible for some of the tasks previously carried out by his supervisor. The intent is invariably to create jobs which are less divided up, which cover a greater range of tasks, and which provide more opportunities for decision making and self-management. Another example occurs where an employee may receive instructions on his production for a week ahead. He may then be given responsibility to plan his work within that schedule. This is a transfer of authority and responsibility from the management/control function down to the worker himself.

Autonomous work group
Here the unit for job design is the whole group rather than the individual members of the group. The group becomes responsible for its own self management once output and quality targets have been agreed. The role of the supervisor is thus changed drastically. Because the group is concerned with a whole process, involving a range of tasks and skills, a greater opportunity exists for each member to experience a variety of tasks; also, because of required interaction and the sharing of tasks a mutually supportive climate is usually engendered and valued. Perhaps a good way of describing an autonomous work group is as a complex task managed with a simple organization rather than the more usual simplified task managed with a highly complex organization.

The essential principle is the formal grouping of people and machinery along a production line, around homogeneous tasks and covering a total task. It is important that the group should be organized *along* a production line, not 'across the grain' over several lines. Also important are the removal of restraints to group functioning such as excessive noise and rigid work stations. Where production groups are used in direct manufacturing, it is often advantageous to include various auxiliary tasks in their work. Continuous checking of variables, lubrication and minor repairs can be efficiently handled by the production group itself.

Semi-autonomous work group
The main difference between this approach and a fully-autonomous work group is that the supervisor retains overall responsibility for the performance of the group, rather than leaving everything to the group itself. But the tasks still remain structured around the principle of group working, with mutual sharing of roles, multi-skilling and a larger degree of internal self management.

What has emerged most strongly from the experiences and research of the last 20 years is that job design or enrichment is an important motivational strategy; it needs to be applied not as an approach in isolation but rather as part and parcel of a total approach. In short, it cannot be separated from such factors as payment systems; promotion, development and training; technological constraints; working conditions and the kind of management style exercised.

Conclusion

The most demanding and difficult part of the manager's job is in the one area of responsibility common to all managers, managing people and relationships, and it is this more than anything which determines success or failure. Our aim has been to provide an opportunity for self development in the awareness, skills and knowledge necessary for the successful management of people at work.

Increasingly, we live in a world where the rate of change is accelerating, goals are becoming more varied and perhaps conflicting and where forms other than structural authority are becoming important. All these increase the complexity of managing people and makes this crucial aspect of the manager's job harder.

There are no simple prescriptions or panaceas to the successful management of people. It is a far too complex and dynamic business for that. We have quite deliberately not advocated particular theories as 'cure-alls': rather, our central thrust is towards diagnosis and analysis. The thoughts we have discussed are vehicles to help you along this route.

We believe that, in common with other aspects of management, the management of people is more concerned with the problem solving/solution cycle calling for the skills and knowledge of awareness, analysis, diagnosis, decision, action and effect. A crucial aspect of awareness is awareness of self—the part of me that forms the equation with other people and the problem—and it is for this reason that some of the activities in the book have been designed to increase your self awareness.

We hope that you can now make better answers to some of the questions we posed earlier.

What am I doing when I manage?
How do I manage other people?

Do I understand myself and others?
How can I help people learn and develop?
What creates good and bad relationships?
How do I influence others?
How do I handle conflict?
What is communication without words?
What helps success in face to face contact?
What makes meetings effective?
How can a group's performance be influenced?
How should change be handled?
What helps people to work well?

Managing people and relationships can be a most rewarding part of the job, not only in terms of the task results achieved, but through the satisfaction of all the people involved, including yourself. It is, too, a fascinating business.

Bibliography

These book references are to works which have formed the basis of some parts of *Human Aspects of Management*, or are recommended further reading.

ARGYLE M, *Bodily Communication*, Methuen, 1975
ARGYLE M, *The Psychology of Interpersonal Relations*, Penguin, 1967
BACK K & K, *Assertiveness at Work*, McGraw-Hill, 1982
BARKER D, *T.A. and Training*, Gower Press, 1980
BERNE E, *Games People Play*, Penguin, 1977
BIDDLE D S, HUTTON G, 'Towards a Tolerance Theory of Worker Adaptation', *Human Relations*, 29, 1976
BLAKE R R, SHEPARD H A, MOUTON J S, *Managing Intergroup Conflict in Industry*, Gulf Publishing, 1968
BOLTON G M, *Testing in Selection Decisions*, NFER/NELSON, 1983
BURNS T, STALKER G M, *The Management of Innovation*, Tavistock, 1961
CHILD J, *Organization: A Guide to Problems and Practice*, Harper and Row, 1977
CLARK N, et al, *Unfinished Business*, Gower Press, 1984
CUMMINGS L L, SCOTT W E, *Organizational Behaviour and Human Performance*, Richard D Irwin and The Dorsey Press, 1969
EYSENCK H J, *Fact and Fiction in Psychology*, Penguin, 1965
ETZIONI A, *Modern Organizations*, Prentice-Hall, 1964
FAST J, *Body Language*, Pan, 1970
FOX A, *Industrial Sociology and Industrial Relations*, Paper No. 3, Royal Commission on Trade Unions, HMSO, 1966
HANDY C, *Understanding Organizations*, Penguin, 1986
HARRIS F A, *I'm OK, You're OK*, Pan, 1976
HERZBERG, M, *Work and the Nature of Man*, Staples Press, 1966
HIGHAM M, *Coping with Interviews*, New Opportunity Press, 1982
HUSSEY D E, LANGHAM, M J, *Corporate Planning: The Human Factor*, Pergamon Press, 1979

HUTTON G, *Thinking about Organization*, Tavistock Publications, 1972

KELLEY C, *Assertion Training – A Facilitator's Guide*, University Associates, 1979

LORSCH J, BAUGHMAN J, REECE J, MINTZBERG H, *Understanding Management*, Harper and Row, 1978

JAMES M, JONGEWOOD D, *Born to Win*, Addison Wesley, 1971

MARGERISON C, *Influencing Organizational Change*, Institute of Personnel Management, 1978

MASLOW A H, *Motivation and Personality*, Harper and Row, 1970

McCLELLAND D C, *The Achieving Society*, Van Nostrand, 1961

McGREGOR D, *The Human Side of Enterprise*, Penguin, 1987

McKAY M, et al., *Messages, The Communications Skills Book*, New Harbinger Publications

MORRIS D, *Manwatching*, Jonathan Cape, 1977

OLDCORN R, *Management. A Fresh Approach*, Pan, 1982

PATERSON T T, *Management Theory*, Business Publications, 1966

PFEIFFER J W, JONES J E, *Handbook of Structured Experiences in Human Relations*, University Associates, 1978

PUGH D S, et al., *Writers on Organisations*, Penguin, 1986

ROSE M, *Industrial Behaviour*, Penguin, 1988

SCHEIN E H, *Organisational Psychology*, Prentice-Hall, 1980

SCHEIN E H, *Process Consultation*, Addison Wesley, 1969

TORRINGTON D, HALL L, *Personnel Management: A New Approach*, Prentice-Hall, 1987

VROOM V H, DECI E L (eds), *Management and Motivation*, Penguin Modern Management Readings, 1970

WOODWARD J, *Management and Technology*, HMSO, 1970